Higher education and manpower planning

Higher education and manpower planning
A comparative study of planned and market economies

O. Fulton, A. Gordon, G. Williams

A joint project undertaken by the
ILO and the UNESCO European Centre
for Higher Education (CEPES)

International Labour Office   Geneva

Copyright © International Labour Organisation 1982

Publications of the International Labour Office enjoy copyright under Protocol 2 of the Universal Copyright Convention. Nevertheless, short excerpts from them may be reproduced without authorisation, on condition that the source is indicated. For rights of reproduction or translation, application should be made to the Publications Branch (Rights and Permissions), International Labour Office, CH-1211 Geneva 22, Switzerland. The International Labour Office welcomes such applications.

ISBN 92-2-102973-5

First published 1982

The designations employed in ILO publications, which are in conformity with United Nations practice, and the presentation of material therein do not imply the expression of any opinion whatsoever on the part of the International Labour Office concerning the legal status of any country or territory or of its authorities, or concerning the delimitation of its frontiers.
The responsibility for opinions expressed in signed articles, studies and other contributions rests solely with their authors, and publication does not constitute an endorsement by the International Labour Office of the opinions expressed in them.

ILO publications can be obtained through major booksellers or ILO local offices in many countries, or direct from ILO Publications, International Labour Office, CH-1211 Geneva 22, Switzerland. A catalogue or list of new publications will be sent free of charge from the above address.

Printed by the International Labour Office, Geneva, Switzerland

TABLE OF CONTENTS

	Page
PREFACE	i
INTRODUCTION	1
CHAPTER 1: The growth of higher education since the Second World War	3
CHAPTER 2: The changing role of higher education in Europe	14
CHAPTER 3: Theoretical issues	23
CHAPTER 4: A formal model	37
CHAPTER 5: Making forecasts of qualified manpower requirements	44
CHAPTER 6: Converting manpower forecasts to educational plans	64
CHAPTER 7: The implementation of manpower-based plans for higher education	83
CHAPTER 8: The content of higher education	102
CHAPTER 9: The role of lifelong education	107
CHAPTER 10: Woman power	114
CHAPTER 11: An appraisal of the current situation	121
REFERENCES I: The country case studies	124
REFERENCES II: Other studies	125

PREFACE

Highlighting the links between education, the labour market and employment policy has been a major field of enquiry conducted under the ILO's World Employment Programme. At the same time UNESCO and, more particularly its European Centre for Higher Education (CEPES) has been concerned with obtaining a better understanding of the problems connected with the development of education which seeks to achieve mutual adjustments between the manpower requirements of the economy and the social demand for places in higher education.

This convergence of interest, though imbedded in different viewpoints, gave rise to a joint project of the ILO and CEPES focussing on the interrelationship of higher education and manpower planning in seven European countries comprising three market and four centrally planned economies. The country studies formed the basis for the preparation of a comparative investigation which within a common framework reviews different countries' experiences in the application of various manpower planning approaches and techniques to educational planning, especially its higher-level component. The results of this investigation are the subject of this document which was prepared by O. Fulton, W. Gordon and G. Williams, all of the Institute of Research and Development in Post Compulsory Education of the University of Lancaster, UK.

Beyond the value of this document as a penetrating and lucidly written account of the current issues experienced in the countries under review in the twin fields of manpower and educational planning and of the ways and means followed to deal with these issues, there is a more general meritorious feature of the investigation. This is the critical, but at the same time constructive, appraisal of the actual and potential usefulness as well as the limitations of manpower planning in general, and in relation to educational planning in particular.

Seen from this angle, the most important parts of the investigation consist of the discussion of the raison-d'être of manpower planning for higher education and of the various approaches, stages and techniques of application. This discussion starts with a presentation of the case for and against manpower planning for higher education. This is followed by the introduction of a formal model which, in turn, sets the point of departure for a detailed review of the various manpower forecasting techniques which have been applied, their pros and cons and the conversions of the forecasts made with these techniques into operational educational plans. The instruments used to implement manpower-based plans for higher education and the constraints met are further areas of inquiry. Special attention is then given to a few important subjects which have been largely neglected in past manpower planning exercises: the content of higher education, the role of life-long education and participation of women. The document terminates with a brief assessment of the present situation and outlook in the countries concerned.

In setting out clearly the various approaches, stages and techniques of manpower forecasting operations for educational planning and in discussing in detail all the factors that need to be taken into account to make full use of the potential of the manpower planning instrument as well as to avoid its pitfalls, the study acquires certain traits of a manual on manpower planning combined with practical illustrations provided by the seven country studies. Manpower planning guidelines of this type are in short supply and this is why the document is published under an ILO series of documents which is designed to underpin a longer-term programme of technical cooperation to assist developing countries in upgrading their capacity in manpower planning and labour market information[1]. This over-all programme is likely to benefit a great deal from the joint ILO/UNESCO investigation presented in this document. Dealing with the problem of the increasing complexity of the relationship between manpower requirements and higher education, which pertains to the programme of UNESCO with respect to the promotion of the role of higher education in society, the study will be of interest to higher education authorityes, managers and planners, not only in the European region represented by the seven case studies, but also in other regions of the world.

A special word of acknowledgement is due to Mr. P. Melvyn of the ILO's Manpower Policies Branch and Mr. Keller, former Director of the UNESCO European Centre for Higher Education. They initiated, prepared and monitored the many activities which led to the conduct of the seven country studies and the publication of the present document.

A. Øfjord, Director, European Centre for Higher Education, (CEPES), Bucharest.	L. Richter, Chief, Manpower Policies Branch, Employment and Development Department, ILO, Geneva.

---

[1] ILO, Strengthening manpower and employment information for decision-making - A summary account of a new programme of technical cooperation (Geneva, 1981).

INTRODUCTION

In most industrialised countries, higher education underwent a very rapid expansion during the 1960s and early 1970s. The great increase in enrolments occurred mainly as a result of an inter-action between two different pressures - the needs of economies for highly qualified manpower and increasing social demand for places in higher education. This expansion shows some signs of having slowed down in recent years, during which time there has been growing evidence of imbalances between the supply of and demand for various categories of qualified personnel. In the market economies these imbalances are revealed in extended periods of job search, declining salary differentials in favour of the highly qualified and the under-, mis- or unemployment of graduates. These "mismatches", as they are sometimes called, have led to a widening gap between the aspirations and expectations of students and graduates and the job opportunities open to them.

In the centrally planned economies these difficulties have to some extent been avoided mainly as a result of their efforts to plan higher education on the basis of the manpower needs of the economy. This has in practice normally led to a rather slower growth rate than that of countries which rely on "social demand", but has also meant that all students can normally expect to have a job waiting for them when they graduate. However, the social demand for places in higher education is often very high, with applicants outnumbering places available in most subject areas. In addition, despite the application of manpower forecasting techniques to higher education, rapid scientific and technological developments, economic growth and structural changes in various branches of the economy have led to some difficulties of adjustment.

In order to understand better the common problems of planning higher education in accordance with society's needs in both centrally planned and market economies, a joint project was undertaken by the International Labour Office (ILO) and the UNESCO European Centre for Higher Education (CEPES), Bucharest, as part of the World Employment Programme, on the links between higher education and manpower planning in seven European countries. The countries which participated in this study, and for which working papers were prepared by national experts, were the Federal Republic of Germany, the German Democratic Republic, Hungary, the Netherlands, Poland, Romania and Sweden.[1] This book aims, mainly on the basis of these country reports, to draw out the links between higher education and manpower planning within a comparative framework and to review different countries' experiences in planning higher education, so that the knowledge gained over long periods by individual countries can be shared amongst all those interested in policy and planning activities in this area.

The countries involved have in the past sharply differed in their attitudes towards planning higher education on the basis of manpower needs. As we shall see, however, there is some evidence to suggest that the centrally planned economies of socialist Europe and the market economies of Western Europe are beginning to

---

[1] See References I.

converge in their choice of solutions to the structural and social difficulties which they are experiencing. The pressures of social demand and the inevitable difficulties of forecasting manpower needs a long time in advance are causing the centrally planned countries to review their planning procedures. Imbalances in the supply of and demand for qualified manpower, coupled with the high costs involved in providing places in higher education on the basis of social demand have led some market economies to examine seriously the possibility of linking at least some parts of the higher education system to the known needs of the economy. All countries have attempted, through counselling and guidance procedures, to make students better informed in their choice of courses of study and the careers to which their studies lead.

By reviewing the experiences of four centrally planned and three market economies, this book attempts to bring together varied conceptions of the planning function and to examine in detail the developments in planning higher education which are being devised to meet changing economic, social and technological circumstances.

CHAPTER 1

The growth of higher education since the Second World War

The period of roughly 30 years since the end of the Second World War has been marked throughout Europe by industrial and economic reconstruction and growth, by rising populations, rising standards of living and, perhaps more than anything else, by rising educational standards. All of these factors are interconnected in complex ways and one of the aims of this book is to describe the extent to which some of these connections have been formalised and used as a basis for planning. Before embarking on any discussion of the theory or practice of planning procedures, however, we shall briefly describe the growth of higher education in Europe, both in terms of numbers of students and of the institutions in which they study.

Figure 1.1 shows the growth of higher education since the Second World War in schematic form, and places Europe and the USSR, as a whole, within a world-wide context. It can be seen that student numbers in Europe have grown at rates very close to those for the whole developed world and indeed at rates similar to those for the other sectors of the developed world, North America and Oceania. In each case we see the characteristic rising curve, culminating in a doubling of enrolments in the early sixties. This is followed by a decline in the rate of growth in the late sixties and a further decline in the early seventies. Descriptions of this phenomenon are commonplace; explanations range from discussions of the ubiquity of the S curve in the growth of social institutions to sociologically and economically complex accounts of the factors which may affect demand. Some of these explanations will be discussed later. (It should be noted, however, that whatever its more subtle causes, the high growth rate of the sixties was partly fuelled by population changes, most countries having experienced a "baby boom" in the early post-war years: in the Netherlands, for example, about half of university expansion can be explained by population growth (Ritzen, 1977).) For the moment, however, it may be less useful to inquire into causation than to discuss some of the features that have accompanied the post-war expansion of numbers.

At the risk of superficiality, one can say that high growth rates tend to have consequences at three levels - societal, system-wide and institutional. At the societal level the growth of any one state-supported activity cannot continue indefinitely at a faster rate than over-all economic growth, since there must be a limit to the amount of resources that can be expended on one particular endeavour. Secondly, a continual growth in the output of highly trained manpower presupposes an equivalent growth in the employment opportunities for such manpower (though not necessarily in the jobs traditionally performed by graduates) - or the alternatives of emigration or unemployment. However, in the early years of educational expansion - and, indeed, until the rate of growth began to decline - some of the increased output from higher education was in practice absorbed by the extra staffing needs of educational institutions themselves.

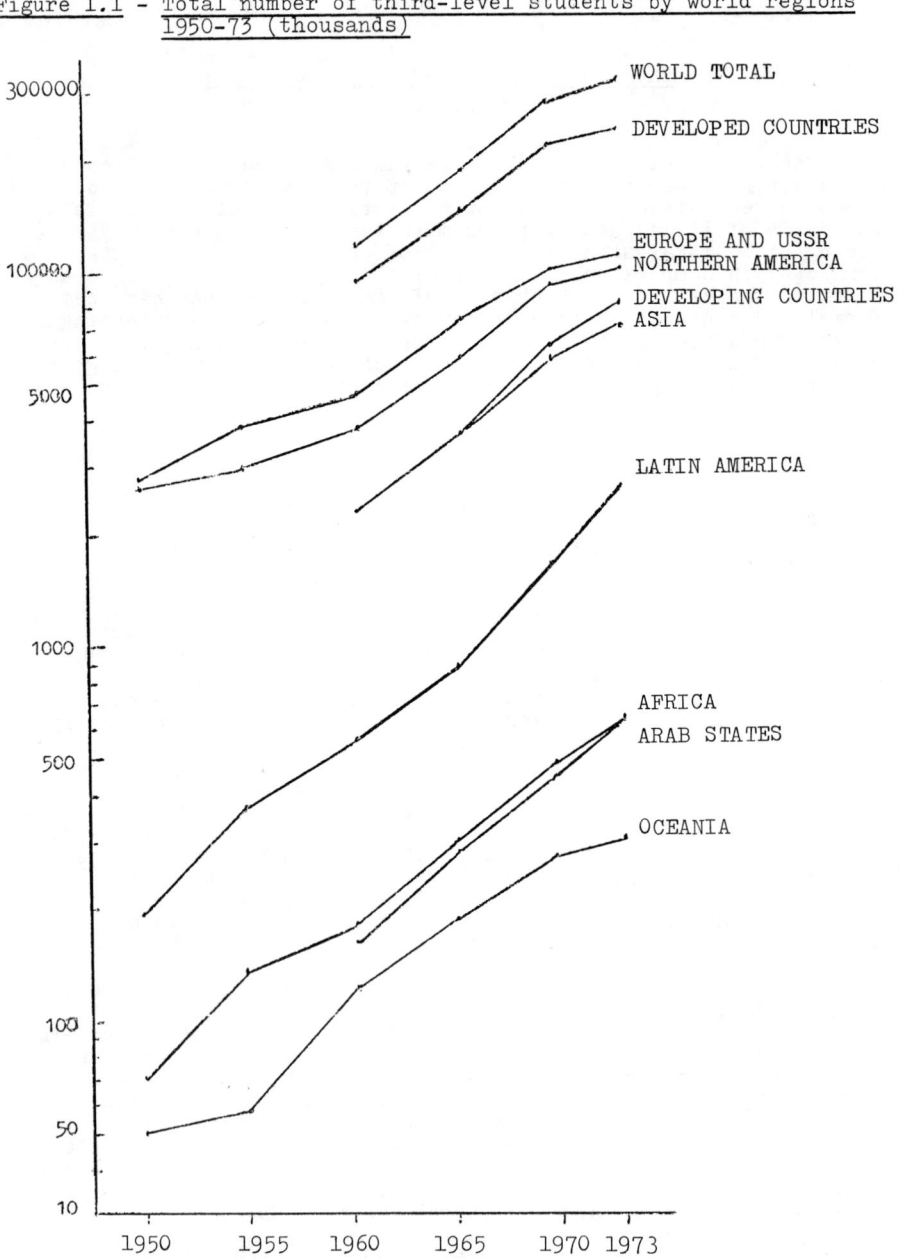

Figure 1.1 - Total number of third-level students by world regions 1950-73 (thousands)

Source: UNESCO (1965); UNESCO (1975).

At what we have called the system-wide level, another set of problems has emerged. In the post-war period, nearly all European countries have transformed their institutions of higher education from autonomous or semi-autonomous enterprises, with considerable freedom of financial management and of control of access, to members of a system, at least partly centrally planned and financed and bearing a very different relationship to the State (and to each other) from that of the university ideal of previous centuries. This transformation has, of course, taken place to different extents and with different degrees of deliberateness, in different countries. But there are now no countries in Europe for whom the concept of academic freedom still gives universities an unqualified right to determine either the size of their intake or their sources and level of finance.

This development is a natural enough consequence of the increased size and economic significance of higher education but it can be seen as part of a series of consequences of expansion, some of which are more problematic. Trow (1974) has pointed out that the growth of higher education leads inevitably to qualitative rather than merely quantitative change, and has described the postwar period in Europe as a change from "élite" to "mass" higher education. When more than a small proportion of the age group has access to higher education, the system and its institutions inevitably change character in many different ways. These changes generally include both the origins and the destinations of graduates, the amount of resources expended on teaching and hence the kind and quality of instruction and, indeed, the structure of higher education institutions. Sooner or later, it becomes impossible to continue to expand universities of the "élite" type, and new institutional forms develop, whether non-university types of higher education or "comprehensive" higher education institutions. Thus, in all seven countries that are studied here, there have been major structural changes in the over-all shape of the higher education system, accompanied by internal changes in nearly all pre-existing universities and colleges.

In this chapter we have chosen to emphasise the similarities between the seven countries, since we feel that, while solutions to problems may differ, there is much in common in the problems which are faced by all seven. But it must be acknowledged that not only are solutions quite sharply different (in particular, the use of the techniques of manpower planning with which this book is primarily concerned); so, too, are some of the aims of the various societies as they affect higher education. These aims will be discussed in Chapter 2 but it is worth reminding the reader that there are differences on at least two levels. On the one hand, broad political objectives, such as a reliance on planning rather than on the mechanisms of the market, or an emphasis on social equality as opposed to individual achievement, can have practical implications, even if the universal forces of modernisation and expansion tend to mitigate their impact to some extent. But more immediate political objectives have undeniable and immediate effects. For example, some of the socialist economies of Eastern Europe have been anxious to avoid creating rigid graduate/non-graduate distinctions within their enterprises. Given the technical requirements of modern management, those skilled workers who are selected for promotion often need to acquire additional academic skills. This has led these countries to place much greater emphasis than in Western Europe on part-time and evening study for adults within higher education. Other examples of what may be called middle-level policy differences will be seen in the pages that follow.

We turn first, however, to look in more detail at the growth of enrolments in Europe since the Second World War. Table 1.1 is intended to give a broad impression of the growth in enrolments within each country and not provide a rigorous cross-national comparison.[1] Indeed, it has to be emphasised that each of the seven countries started from quite different positions. The level of institutional provision which existed in 1950 varied very substantially; in some countries the war had almost destroyed both the buildings and the staff which were available for post-secondary education. It must also be remembered that in the post-war period European countries varied substantially in the amount of resources at their disposal for education at any level, and that the other levels of the educational system showed perhaps even greater disparities between one country and the next. Indeed, several of the newly socialist states had inherited substantial levels of illiteracy, which became one of their first priorities for educational reform. In Romania, for example, more than one-quarter of the population was illiterate in 1944.[2] When comparing growth rates, it must also be remembered that table 1.1 takes no account of population differences, either as they affected the over-all numbers of potential students in any one year, or indeed as their fluctuations[3] might affect the possibilities for expansion.

Table 1.1 shows that if measured by UNESCO's figures, growth rates have ranged over the past quarter century from roughly threefold (Romania) to well over tenfold (German Democratic Republic). In most of these countries, there can have been no comparable period of sustained growth in the earlier history of higher education, and there has certainly never been one on such a scale. In the seven countries taken together, there were some 470,000 students in third-level education in 1950 and approximately 2,320,000 in 1974. Thus, places were found for nearly 2 million extra students during the post-war boom. Indeed, by the seventies, both the Federal Republic of Germany and Poland were each enrolling more students than all seven countries combined in 1950.

---

[1] Figures supplied in the seven ILO/CEPES studies are given first, followed by the figures for "third-level education" reported to UNESCO over the years and published in the UNESCO Statistical Yearbook and/or in the UNESCO publication, Education Statistics - Latest Year Available. As UNESCO warns, differences in criteria for enumeration and indeed structural differences "impair international comparability". Thus, not even the UNESCO figures, and still less those from the seven case studies, can be taken as affording simple superficial comparisons between one country and another. Indeed, in some cases a comparison between the two sets of figures for the same country shows marked discrepancies which may serve as a warning. With these reservations, however, table 1.1 may be used to show the rough scale of growth within each country.

[2] Pestisanu et al., 1977.

[3] For example, the age cohort eligible for admission in the German Democratic Republic in 1960 was about twice the size of that in 1966 (Sachse, 1977), as a result of the sharp drop in births in the final years of the Second World War.

Table 1.1 - Total enrolments in post-secondary education, 1950-75

	(a) ILO/CEPES		(b) UNESCO	
	Universities	Other higher education	Third-level education	
F.R. Germany	N	N	N	Index (1950:100)
1950		128 000*	162 577	100
1955			193 852	119
1960		240 000	241 686	179
1965		300 000	373 099	229
1970	353 161	146 666	503 819	310
1975	557 422	283 335	840 757	517

* 1952 figure

German D.R.

1951			27 822	100
1955	76 700		60 148	216
1960	101 800	(126 000)*	69 129	248
1965	108 300	111 800	220 591	793
1970	138 700	164 600	303 141	1 090
1974	136 400	154 300	306 783	1 103

* In the early sixties the "colleges" were modified and restructured to exclude UNESCO second-level studies which they had previously undertaken (Sachse, 1977, p. 5).

Hungary

1950	25 981	6 520	29 997	100
1955	41 862	3 569	45 007	150
1960	37 267	7 290	44 545	148
1965	57 482	36 475	93 957	313
1970	47 218	33 318	80 536	268
1974	52 775	51 331	103 390	345

Netherlands

1950	27 736		61 036	100
1955	29 642		75 512	119
1960	40 727	65 495	105 995	174
1965	64 409	85 210	152 748	250
1970	103 382	126 077	231 167	379
1974	127 669*	167 892+	264 297	433

* 1976 figure   + 1975 figure

	(a) ILO/CEPES		(b) UNESCO	
	Universities	Other higher education	Third-level education	

Poland   Index
                                                                          (1950:100)

	Intra-mural	Extra-mural		
1950	117 506	7 590	117 506*	100*
1955	120 143	37 322	120 143*	102*
1960	111 342	54 345	111 342*	95*
1965	152 362	99 502	339 508+	(289)+
1970	209 846	120 943	397 897+	(339)+
1974	258 149	168 552	521 899+	(444)+

* Excluding extra-mural courses
+ Including extra-mural courses

Romania

1950	52 007	53 007	100
1955		77 633	146
1960		71 989	136
1965		130 614	246
1970		151 885	287
1974	152 728	152 728	288

Sweden

1950	7 000*	7 000*	16 887	100
1955			22 647	134
1960	46 000+		36 909	219
1965			77 752	460
1970	122 000		141 218	836
1974			128 879	763

* "Early 1950s" figures   + 1962 figures

Sources: ILO/CEPES: FRG: Hüfner et al., 1977; GDR: Sachse, 1977; Hungary: Ivan, 1977; Netherlands: Ritzen, 1977; Poland: Kluczynski and Jozefowicz, 1977; Romania: Pestisanu et al., 1977; Sweden: Bergendal, 1977; UNESCO, 1960, UNESCO, 1975 and UNESCO, 1977.

It is also noticeable from table 1.1 that in five out of the seven countries (the exceptions being the Federal Republic of Germany and the Netherlands) expansion took place at the fastest rate in the early sixties. In Sweden, Poland, Hungary and the German Democratic Republic, the availability of places more than doubled in the five years between 1960 and 1965. But in most countries expansion has slowed substantially in the seventies. Indeed, in Romania it has virtually ceased; both sectors of higher education have contracted in the German Democratic Republic since 1970 (Sachse, 1977); and there has been a marked contraction in Sweden. Such uneven bursts of growth, often followed by stability or even contraction, must inevitably bring problems in the internal functioning of educational institutions. And, depending on the closeness of the relationship between education and the labour market in the country concerned, such fluctuations can serve as a cause, or at least may be taken as an indicator, of strains in the relationship of supply and demand in the market for highly qualified manpower.

The figures given above, for total enrolments and for rates of growth in enrolments, tell us something about the way in which higher education has grown in importance in individual countries in Europe but rather less about its absolute importance, either now or in the past. We shall discuss its financial and economic significance later; at this point it may be useful to examine its direct impact on educational opportunities and on educational achievement by looking at participation rates. These can be measured in various forms. Here, we look at three methods of measurement, where available: crude participation ratios, age group or cohort participation rates, and education levels among the adult population.

The first of these, derived from UNESCO statistics, is shown in table 1.2. Like all such summary rates, the crude participation ratio must be used with caution. It shows the total enrolment in third-level education, regardless of the age of students, as a percentage of the total population aged between 20 and 24. It does not, therefore, take account of population fluctuations within the 20-24 group, of different ages of attendance and, perhaps most crucially, of different lengths of courses of study between one country and the next.[1] With these reservations, however, it can be seen that ratios range from 28 per cent in the German Democratic Republic, through roughly 20 per cent in Sweden, the Federal Republic of Germany and the Netherlands, to 15 per cent in Poland, 11 per cent in Hungary and 8 per cent in Romania.

More informative, however, are the figures provided by the ILO/CEPES country studies on participation rates, either for age cohorts or among those of a specified age. Once again, there are problems of comparability: different authors use a variety of methods of calculation. Nevertheless, among the market economies of Western Europe, in the Netherlands approximately 13 per cent of

---

[1] For example, if courses in country "A" normally last for two years, compared with four years in country "B", an enrolment ratio of 10 per cent in "A" may present exactly the same opportunity for a 20-year old to participate as a ratio of 20 per cent in "B".

males and 7 per cent of females (figures for the sexes are not summed) aged 20 - the age at which attendance is highest - were attending university or higher vocational education in 1971 (Ritzen, 1977, page 14). For each sex, this is approximately double the proportion in 1958. In the Federal Republic of Germany, by contrast, 9.6 per cent of 22 year olds - the age of highest attendance - (or 11 per cent of males and 8 per cent of females) were enrolled in universities, technical universities, or teacher training colleges in 1975 (Hüfner et al. 1977, page 8). The comparable figure for 1952 was 2.4 per cent. Finally, in Sweden, in the "late 1960s", 21 per cent of 20 year olds were enrolled in universities and colleges, compared with 4 per cent in the "early 1950s" (computed from Bergendal, 1977, page 12). These figures represent quite a wide variation in participation rates among young people at the age of normal university attendance, though it should be noted that the figure for the Federal Republic of Germany, which appears to have the lowest participation rate, does not include the fast increasing number of students attending non-university forms of higher education. It is also clear that the opportunities for young people to enrol in higher education have increased quite dramatically in the post-war period in all three countries.

Table 1.2 - Gross enrolment ratios* in third-level education in seven European countries: latest figures available

	Date	Ratio %
F.R. Germany	1973	18
German D.R.	1973	28
Hungary	1973	11
Netherlands	1971	21
Poland	1973	15
Romania	1973	8
Sweden	1973	22

* The total enrolment of students of all ages in third-level education as a proportion of the population of the age group 20-24.

Source: UNESCO Statistical Yearbook, 1975, table 3.2.

Among the centrally planned economies of Eastern Europe, the German Democratic Republic enrolled, in the period 1971 to 1974, 10 per cent of a "typical age cohort", in university courses and another 12.5 per cent in colleges of various kinds (medical, teacher training and technical). Moreover, planners predicted that another 10.5 per cent of this cohort would in due course undertake studies in tertiary education by correspondence (Sachse, 1977, page 3). In Poland, where figures are given on a basis closer to that of UNESCO, students in higher education constituted in 1974-75 6.7 per cent of young people aged 19-24: an increase from 3.9 per cent in 1960-61 (Kluczynski and Jozefowicz, 1977, page 10); but 12 per cent of young people aged 19-23 are described as achieving higher education at some time in their lives. Finally, in Hungary in 1970 students participating in day-course higher education constituted 6.3 per cent of the total population "of corresponding age", compared with 3.4 per cent in 1950 (Ivan, 1977, page 9). In the centrally planned economies, too, therefore, there has been both a considerable growth in opportunities in higher education and quite substantial differences between one country and another - differences which can probably be attributed largely to the lasting effects of different levels of economic development in the post-war period.

This expansion of higher education has obviously increased the proportion of graduates in the adult population. In Hungary, the percentage of graduates in the labour force has risen from 1.9 per cent in 1949 to 5.1 per cent in 1970 (Ivan, 1977, pages 1-2). In the German Democratic Republic, the labour force in 1971 contained 4.4 per cent university graduates and another 7.4 per cent technical college graduates, compared with 2.4 per cent from universities and 4.3 per cent from technical colleges in 1962 (Sachse, 1977, page 19). In Poland, figures are available only for the educational level of the whole population, employed or not, aged 15 years or over: 3.1 per cent of adults were university graduates in 1974. But about 6 per cent of those aged between 25 and 39 were graduates (Kluczynski and Jozefowicz, 1977, page 14). In the Netherlands, 5.0 per cent of males in the labour force were graduates from university or other forms of higher education in 1960; by 1973 this proportion had risen to 9.8 per cent. For employed females, the comparable figures are 4.1 per cent and 9.3 per cent (Ritzen, 1977, page 42). In all these European countries, therefore, it could be argued that graduates are no longer a tiny élite but a numerically significant section of the labour force and, of course, the steady growth in enrolments means that their presence is most noticeable among the younger employed.

We suggested above that one of the almost universal consequences of the growth of higher education seems to be structural reform. The pressures of growth and differentiation seem to lead to three developments: an expansion of non-university higher education; later, a tendency to merge university and non-university forms into more flexible, comprehensive institutions; and an increased emphasis on part-time higher education. Part-time studies serve in some cases merely as an alternative to conventional full-time enrolment for young people who wish to enter the labour market sooner, but they are also part of a general tendency to switch the emphasis in higher education away from the traditional clientele of young people with high secondary school qualifications and towards a wider, more adult market, at least part of which holds fewer traditional qualifications. The place of continuing education in manpower planning is discussed in Chapter 9. Here, we shall illustrate these general trends by briefly describing the structure of higher and further education in the seven countries under study.

In the Federal Republic of Germany, 18 universities or technical universities constituted the whole of higher education in 1950. Since that time, the number of university-type institutions has increased to 49. But teacher-training colleges are now counted as part of higher education, as are a large and increasing number of technical colleges. The most recent development is the creation of "comprehensive academies" (Gesamthochschulen), combining the function of university and technical college under one roof. However, students in higher education in the Federal Republic of Germany are predominantly full-time with evening and correspondence studies assuming little importance. In the Netherlands, universities have been, and still are, distinguished from the sector known as higher vocational education - including a large variety of specialised professional and subprofessional training colleges.

But it is now government policy that these two sectors should converge in administrative structure, curricula and by interchanging students, with a view to ultimate merger. In Sweden, in place of two post-war universities there are now six and here, too, there exists a variety of specialised but by no means always lower status teaching institutions. Under the "U68" proposals, however, some of which have already been implemented, Swedish higher education is being converted into a comprehensive, unified structure, centrally financed but regionally administered, with six regional organisations each absorbing one university and the full range of higher and further education institutions in the locality. Indeed, higher education in Sweden is to be decentralised and reconstituted into a multilocational structure, with branches offering studies at all levels in every town. There are already substantial opportunities for highly flexible part-time study arrangements.

In centrally planned economies, as we have seen, considerably greater emphasis is placed on part-time and extra-mural higher education, for a variety of political and manpower reasons. As to the formal institutional structure in which full- and part-time studies take place, Poland has seen a fluctuation between a two-tier and a single-tier model - a binary system was introduced in 1948, abandoned in the late 1950s, and partially restored in 1964. It would perhaps not be unfair to see this fluctuation as exemplifying a conflict between the social and economic demands being placed on the higher education system. Future plans in Poland will involve the creation of comprehensive institutions - comprehensive not so much in the sense of combining studies at different academic levels but in combining studies in different educational cycles. In the future, far more emphasis will be placed on continuing and recurrent education for those needing retraining as well as those who have not previously attended higher education. Hungary possesses a four-tier system, though there is a basic two-part division between university level and college level studies. Encompassed in the university level are a large number of specialised, monotechnic universities. In the post-war period large numbers of new technical colleges were founded at a rate which was afterwards deemed to have been excessive; many of these colleges have closed or merged with other institutions. In the future, Hungarian higher education is expected to move towards comprehensive institutions, with universities also providing college level studies within their own walls. The general aim of Hungarian planners is to increase the flexibility of their institutions in the light of their expectation that the educational gap between manual and non-manual workers will narrow.

The German Democratic Republic has perhaps the most traditional structure of higher education within the centrally planned economies. Universities and technical colleges are kept quite separate, although both sectors have grown substantially in the post-war period. (The six traditional universities inherited from the pre-war régime were joined by 19 new "technical universities" and a number of other specialised institutions in the university sector.) The expectation is that the binary system will be preserved but that, in some respects, notably in curricula, the gap between the two types of institution will narrow. Romania possesses a range of institutions providing studies for varying lengths of time. Here, however, universities appear to be distinguished from other institutions such as technical schools by their subject matter, which is academic rather than applied, rather than by the educational level at which they teach. There do not appear to be plans for greater unification of the different institutional types. In all of the centrally planned economies there is a great emphasis on part-time and correspondence education.

The post-war growth of higher education has involved economic costs. In some European countries, real expenditure per student in higher education has been reduced (e.g. the Netherlands), largely as a result of relative shifts in enrolment towards subjects with lower instructional costs (Ritzen, 1977, page 35). In other countries, costs per student have been increased (e.g. the German Democratic Republic), in order to improve the quality of instruction. But the scale of growth in enrolments has meant that total expenditures on higher education have increased, not only in real terms, but also in most countries as a percentage of public expenditure and of national income. In the Netherlands where, according to UNESCO (1975), total expenditure on education amounted to 7.8 per cent of gross national product (GNP) in 1974, expenditure on higher education has increased from 0.38 per cent of GNP in 1950 to over 2.0 per cent in the 1970s (Ritzen, 1977, page 35). In Sweden, total educational expenditure was 7.7 per cent of GNP in 1973 (UNESCO, 1975) and higher education consumed 12.7 per cent of recurrent expenditure on education at all levels, plus an undetermined extra amount for student grants and loans (UNESCO, 1975). In the Federal Republic of Germany, educational expenditure was 4.1 per cent of GNP in 1973 (UNESCO, 1975); in higher education, expenditure represented 0.3 per cent of GNP in 1962, 0.6 per cent in 1961 and 1.3 per cent in 1974 (Hüfner et al., 1977, page 17). Poland and Romania each spent more than 5 per cent of national income on education as a whole (Kluczynski and Jozefowicz, 1977, page 13; Pestisanu et al., 1977, page 9) and, in Romania at least, this share is increasing. In Hungary, which spent 4.6 per cent of net material product (NMP) on education in 1974 (UNESCO, 1975), higher education accounted for 0.43 per cent of national income in 1950; 0.41 per cent in 1960; and 0.64 per cent in 1975 (Ivan, 1977, page 1). Finally, in the German Democratic Republic, education as a whole consumed 5 per cent of national product in 1960 and 5.8 per cent in 1974, but higher education's share dropped from 1.4 per cent to 1.2 per cent (Sachse, 1977, page 16).

We suggested earlier that increases in expenditure on higher education could not be expected to continue indefinitely. This has become increasingly obvious, especially in the market economies after the economic recession of the early 1970s. As Hüfner et al. (1977, pages 33-35) put it:

> It should be noticed that the over-all background for the expansion of public activity during the sixties and, in particular, efforts in the fields of education and science, were substantial gains in real economic growth. At the same time ... (there have been) ... tremendous strains on the economy - and also on public policy - after the onset of the present economic crisis in October 1973. With the recent history of expansion as it is, education and science will a very hard stand in defending their relative position and will encounter serious objections to any further expansion.

In the planned economies also, much of the expansion of higher education has undoubtedly been financed by economic growth and could also be vulnerable to any economic slow-down. In all European countries it seems clear that higher education in the future may be required to prove its value. In the next chapter we turn to the question of what that value might be.

CHAPTER 2

The changing role of higher education in Europe

In order to understand the way in which higher education has grown, it is necessary to examine its functions. Why should increasing numbers of students choose, as we saw in Chapter 1, to prolong their educational careers before entering the labour market? And why should societies choose to spend increasing proportions of their resources on this rather expensive institution, which is accessible to only a minority of young people?

Conceptions of the functions of higher education vary to some extent from one society to another. But although the choice of emphasis may differ, there seems to be agreement - at least at a very broad level of generality - on the range of purposes which might be served by educating people to the higher education level. As Kluczynski and Jozefowicz (1977) put it:

> Education has become the basic condition for economic development, an instrumental factor in personal development and a basic source of human happiness and social well-being

Other commentators would argue that, in relation to economic development, higher education might be better described as "instrumental" rather than "basic", especially perhaps in market economies. But the emphasis on the links between the economic, social and personal advantages of higher education would be almost universally shared.

The economic role of higher education is, of course, the main theme of this book. It is not, however, undisputed. The arguments raised by the "credentialist" view of education are briefly reviewed in Chapter 3; essentially, they depend on the degree to which the content of training within educational institutions is relevant to future employment or is indeed in any way necessary for satisfactory performance in a job. Without anticipating the discussion that follows, it is clear that circumstances vary too much to allow one to reach a simple conclusion for or against "credentialism". Whether participation in higher education actually trains a student either directly or indirectly (that is, in specific technical skills or in more general intellectual development) must depend on the nature of the job in question, on the organisation of teaching, the nature of assessment and the content of the curriculum. All these areas, with the exception of the first, are in principle open to manipulation by educational institutions, and hence by the society that maintains them. In other words, whether or not a doctor or an engineer, for example, receives specific job-related training within higher education is a matter of choice.

If we wish to discover what choices have been made by particular European countries, we cannot produce valid, empirically-based answers without examining the content of specific curricula in detail. (General questions concerning the content of the curriculum are discussed in Chapter 8.) We would also need to investigate the question of "substitutability" of highly qualified manpower - which would require tracing the actual careers in employment of graduates with various qualifications. But we can at least examine the views expressed in various countries about the purposes of higher education and we can also look at their procedures for selection of students and recruitment into the job market. It is clear that in the centrally planned economies higher education is believed to be performing a specific training function. This is why manpower planning is undertaken seriously in these countries and is used to determine the size and pattern of enrolments in higher education. In Poland, for example, "the basic task facing the higher education system (is) the preparation of highly qualified professional personnel. (It) consists, in a planned economy, in ensuring the influx of the number of specialists needed for the reconstruction, transformation and planned economic development of the country" (Kluczynski and Jozefowicz, 1977). In Hungary, "the process of planning higher education is ... closely connected with manpower planning and, within this, with the planning of highly qualified personnel. The determination of the number of students admitted to higher education is based on the concrete targets of the national economic plan" (Ivan, 1977). In Sweden, by contrast, a sharp distinction was made, from the 1930s to the 1960s, between two branches of university study: "with an over-simplification ... it can be said that the expansion of technical, economic, medical and other clearly professionally orientated studies with restricted admission was motivated by the needs of the economy, whereas the open faculties of the universities were intended to meet the individual demand for higher education" (Bergendal, 1977). It should be added, however, that part of the motivation for restricting entry to professional subjects appears to have been not so much to ensure the adequate supply of qualified manpower but to protect the professions from over-supply, and graduates in these subjects from unemployment (Bergendal, 1977). In other market economies, indeed, the latter is seen as the primary purpose of using manpower planning to regulate student enrolments. In the Netherlands, despite a state law dating back to 1876 which appears to place primary emphasis on manpower training, manpower planning has only become fashionable in response to the graduate unemployment of the 1970s (Ritzen, 1977). To summarise, then, the centrally planned economies, by their concentration on manpower planning, strongly endorse the concept of higher education as leading to economic development through the training of skilled manpower. Market economies, on the other hand, although they may also accept the principle, have tended until recently to assume that the operations of the labour market will broadly ensure sufficient skilled manpower for development and have therefore felt able, to a much greater extent, to leave the functions of higher education as a matter to be negotiated in the market place between teachers, students and employers.

This difference can be illustrated by reference to European countries and in particular to the ways in which the balance of subjects taught in universities has changed. In the case of the centrally planned economies, changes in fields of study of university graduates are taken as the end-product of a planning process. The similarity of circumstances of the German Democratic Republic, Hungary, Poland and Romania in the post-war period - a shortage of skilled manpower, combined with the need for industrial development, as an aid to post-war growth or reconstruction - has led to very similar changes in patterns of study. In all four countries, education and industry were seen as primary areas for investment and places were made available in steadily increasing numbers for students preparing for teaching and for those in technological and scientific fields. In contrast, fields such as law showed a very sharp decline in student numbers, while medicine showed a relative decline in its share of students, though absolute numbers of medical graduates were stable or even increased slightly (Ivan, 1977; Sachse, 1977; Kluczynski and Jozefowicz, 1977; Pestisanu et al., 1977). Moreover, temporary increases were made where necessary as, for instance, in the training of agricultural specialists in Hungary, who were needed in large numbers in the early stages of collectivisation of agriculture, followed by "a scaling down of education which was inflated transitionally" (Ivan, 1977).

The market economies, however, present a more complex case. In Sweden, as we have seen, there was a large expansion in the faculties with open admission, whereas the restricted faculties were held to much more modest levels of growth. On the whole, the output from these planned faculties seems to have been adequate to meet demand (indeed, by the sixties the only serious shortages appear to have been in occupations requiring non-university training). It must be remembered, however, that Sweden began the post-war period from a more economically advanced point than most other European countries, and without war damage. In the Netherlands, admissions - and hence expansion - were not controlled until 1972, the year in which a numerus fixus was first introduced. But the relative balance between subjects does not differ greatly from other Western European countries: most of the spectacular growth of the sixties was concentrated in the Netherlands, as it was in Sweden, in the social sciences and in arts subjects. Science, technology and medicine grew much more slowly. In the Federal Republic of Germany, however, what was defined as the undue sluggishness of growth in scientific and technical subjects caused the Government to call for a huge increase in capacity in 1957 (Hüfner et al., 1977). This intervention was combined with measures to provide financial assistance to students and so to increase social demand in these subject areas.

It is not immediately apparent, therefore, that either of the two types of economy have proved more effective in aiding economic growth through the provision of higher education. Given the vast range of differences between the two groups of societies, valid comparisons of the effects of different approaches to higher education are not really possible. Furthermore, as has been pointed out earlier, the apparently growing interest of the market economies in the use of manpower planning probably stems at least as much from the social problems associated with the excess supply of graduates as from any anticipated economic problems connected with under-supply.

If we turn now to the social purposes of higher education, these can be subdivided into two types: those that are desirable for their own sake and those that are pursued primarily as a means to some wider social goal. An example of the first is the social and political development of the population. This is a goal that is endorsed to some extent in most societies but with a somewhat greater degree of specificity and perhaps with more wholeheartedness in the centrally planned economies. In Poland, for example, a future, reformed higher education system will fit the following description, according to Kluczynski and Jozefowicz (1977):

The future socio-political and cultural development of the nation is conditioned by the level of education of society as a whole ... all levels of the educational system are important links in the shaping of man's personality, abilities and habits ... (thus) universal secondary education and the accessibility of higher education will form basic links in shaping the ideological, moral, cultural and intellectual attitudes of a developed socialist society. The generation of intelligentsia educated in higher education schools should be prepared both ideologically and occupationally for creative participation in building the future image of the country.

Moreover,

... schools of higher education, in addition to imparting knowledge, are concerned with forming in their graduates the characteristics of a creative, socially motivated and active personality.

In this area of "social education", Kluczynski and Jozefowicz comment (1977):

At present, this function is performed in the universities by the so-called "ideological" subjects and by youth and social organisations. Not all students are within the range of effective influence on their practical preparation for active participation in socio-political life. In designing the model and preparing the programme for future universities, the following directions of activities should therefore be taken into consideration:

First, efforts should be made to increase the number of students active in student organisations by entrusting them with responsible tasks, thus increasing their participation in the social life of their universities.

Second, consideration should be given to the idea of including in the programme of schools of higher education some form of practical preparation for broadly interpreted political, social and cultural work, sports activities, etc.

Third, the system of student participation in research work in their universities should be so developed and the programme of practical training should be so improved as to make of these forms of activities a school of organisational activities operated by the students themselves.

The educational system in schools of higher education thus outlined would, in fact, be a move from the present system of 'guardianship' toward 'partnership', toward education by making students more active in their work and by increasing the extent of self-government and responsibility for the tasks entrusted to them.

In the market economies, similar goals are often endorsed. For example, the "U68" commission in Sweden mentioned the development of democracy and international understanding through education as appropriate aims for universities. However, Bergendal (1977) points out the impossibility of mechanically converting such generalised, "hazy" goals into precisely defined plans, even supposing that unanimity could be reached on the relative desirability of a series of potentially conflicting aims. But this should not be taken to imply that social goals are meaningless, merely that the gap between them and specific plans may be very large.

However, the type of social goal in which higher education functions as a means can be discussed with somewhat more precision. Here, we refer primarily to the goal of increasing social equality. There is, of course, a vast polemical literature, which there is no space to discuss here, on appropriate definitions and measurements of social inequality, on its causes and on the appropriateness or feasibility of remedial measures. One simple point, however, may be worth making. Much recent discussion, especially in the United States (see Jencks et al., 1972) has turned on the degree to which an individual's educational achievement affects his or her eventual occupational location and hence on whether it makes sense to attempt to achieve greater social equality by controlling or manipulating access to education. But the relationship between education and occupation is, of course, a variable. Centrally planned economies, which follow up their investment in manpower planning with a fairly high degree of control over graduates' occupational choice and over recruitment by enterprises, obviously expect to achieve a fairly close link between education and occupation. For them, therefore, equalising access to education is undoubtedly seen both as a step towards greater efficiency in filling jobs demanding high skills and also as a means towards reducing inequality in society at large. "Intergenerational social mobility is achieved through school studies. Consequently, school is the means of achieving the objective of a more open society" (Ivan, 1977). Secondly, as Jencks and his co-authors point out, education is itself a major consumption good - a point of view which, as we shall see, is shared by the centrally planned economies. Thus, equalising access to education is one way of reducing inequalities in access to consumption goods.

There are, of course, many groups in society which appear to have unequal access to higher education. Some of these, such as those people who do not complete their secondary education, or who score low marks in university entrance examinations, are not necessarily problematic. But two sources of inequality cause concern in almost every European country - sex and socio-economic origin. Sex differences in educational and occupational achievement, which appear to have diminished somewhat in recent years (though at very different rates in different countries) are dealt with as a special issue in Chapter 10. But socio-economic differences are sometimes seen as a more central political concern. They are defined in a variety of ways. In Romania, for example, the primary difference is measured in terms of the urban or rural origins of students. According to Pestisanu et al. (1977), the proportion of full-time students from rural origin increased in Romania from 33 per cent in 1965-66 to 38 per cent in 1974-75, a change which represents a rather larger increase in relative opportunities, since the rural population declined from 66 per cent to 57 per cent in the same period. The view of these authors is that rural origins are no longer a source of restriction on access to higher education. In Hungary, some concern is evidently felt about the better educational facilities available in towns and cities, which may discourage those of rural origin who prefer not to move too far from their homes. But the problem is also posed in terms of parental occupations: admissions to university in

Hungary are no longer formally related to social origins, which had previously been a criterion for preferential admission (for the children of workers). Thus, at least in law, equal opportunity now exists. However, there is a tendency for the children of intellectuals to be disproportionately attracted to intellectual careers and, indeed, for their parents to place extra emphasis on the value of education (Ivan, 1977). Attempts are therefore being made, not to reintroduce preferential quotas, but to create a less stratified secondary school system and to provide extra opportunities for part-time study for those already at work. In the German Democratic Republic, too, comprehensive secondary education (in "general polytechnic schools") up to the age of 16, and part-time and correspondence courses in higher education specially designed for skilled workers, have been introduced for similar reasons (Sachse, 1977).

In Poland, the proportion of students (on full-time, intramural courses in higher education) from workers' families rose from 9 per cent in 1939 to 24 per cent in 1949 and 36 per cent in 1958. By 1967 it had dropped to 26 per cent but has now (1974) reached 38 per cent. The proportion of students from peasant families - 8 per cent in 1939 - rose to 22 per cent after the war but has now declined to 11 per cent. Once again, interpretation of actual opportunities is complicated by the changing occupational structure but part of the decline in opportunities for workers is said to have resulted from the introduction of a tripartite structure of secondary education, of which only one non-vocational sector, qualified pupils for university entrance. Measures aimed at increasing democratisation of access include a comprehensive system of secondary education, approved in principle in 1973 and to be introduced shortly; a system of "social preferentiation" for university entrance, to compensate for inadequate schooling and "the cultural and social disparities which inhibit the chances of school leavers of peasant and worker origin"; and an increasing reliance on correspondence and extra-mural forms of higher education, which generally enrol roughly 80 per cent of their students from those of worker or peasant origin (see Kluczynski and Jozefowicz, 1977). Indeed, within extra-mural higher education, the focus of equalisation of opportunities has shifted from disparities between strata to disparities between generations.

In market economies, measures to increase social equality in access to higher education have, in general, been less specific. Partly, it has been widely believed (as in the centrally planned economies) that inequalities in higher education originate in different choices and opportunities at a much earlier age, and that remedial measures are best concentrated in the secondary or even primary school system. It also appears to be the case that structural reforms of school-level education cannot by themselves eliminate inequality. Partly, however, it has been hoped that the expansion of higher education would in itself have relatively more beneficial effects on opportunities for working-class children, who may have been especially likely to be excluded from élite institutions. This hope appears to have been justified in some countries such as Sweden; less so in others, where working-class enrolment was not originally so low. (In Sweden, the proportion of students from workers' families was about 12 per cent in the early 1950s and 21 per cent in the late 1960s (Bergendal, 1977).) But state intervention has often taken a form not seen in the centrally planned economies, of trying to reduce the opportunity costs for working-class children by universal or means-tested financial assistance. This seems to be a logical strategy where reliance is placed on market mechanisms. However, where subsidies or grants are universally available, even if means-tested, it is often found that middle-class children benefit to a large extent, and little or no "democratisation" may occur.

There is a third, broadly social function of education, which has its counterpart at the individual level. This is, in fact, to meet the demand for higher education expressed by individuals. Individuals may demand higher education both as a means of improving their own position in the occupational structure, that is, as a means of economic self-development, and also as a way to satisfy "non-vocational" cultural needs. In the German Democratic Republic, for example, this latter need is recognised as one to which the State must now respond, as well as to the economic need for highly trained manpower.

The responses of European countries to the "social demand" for higher education have until now been sharply different. Many market economies have until recently regarded enrolment as a right, at least for those who have achieved a standard qualification in secondary education. Among these countries have been the Netherlands, the Federal Republic of Germany and (with the exception of certain faculties specified earlier), Sweden. All of these countries, however, have in the last few years introduced restrictions on entry, in the form of numerus clausus (fixus) in some of the most heavily subscribed or over-crowded faculties. Such restrictions have generally been justified mainly as attempts to preserve the standard of education for those admitted but they have obviously been used to control the costs of providing adequate teaching staff and facilities and to reduce the prospects of graduate unemployment. Other market economies, however, (such as Britain) have resembled the centrally planned economies in being quite prepared to fix limits on enrolment in general, although social demand has always played a substantial part in determining the level of these limits. (It should not be forgotten that demand is never a spontaneous expression of individual wills: in all of the market economies it has proved itself sensitive not only to changing opportunities but also to manipulation by the authorities, for example via changes in tuition fees and student maintenance levels.)

It is not possible here to examine all the ways in which social demand has responded to particular circumstances or indeed the fundamental reasons why demand rose for so many years after the war. All that we can do is to examine the most obvious measures of visible demand in the countries under study. In the case of countries, or subjects within countries, with open enrolment policies, expressed demand can simply be measured by enrolment rates (examples of which have already been given in Chapter 1). Where enrolment is restricted to a fixed number of places, we need to look at rates of application for admission. Among the market economies, the Federal Republic of Germany began to impose restrictions in the late 1960s: the extent to which enrolments were restrained can be seen in the figure of 24,400 applications in medicine for 4,000 available places in 1974-75 (Hüfner et al., 1977). Although it is believed that, up to the present time, total demand has been near to or possibly below the total supply of places (meaning that, while some fields are over-subscribed, others have spare capacity), this situation does not seem likely to continue. Indeed, the number of young people achieving entry qualifications is forecast to rise by over 50 per cent by 1980, whereas an increase in capacity is thought to be unlikely. Thus, the Federal Republic is likely to experience substantial excess social demand in the next few years. (Proposals have been made to try to accommodate all applicants, nevertheless, by shortening the average length of study.) In the Netherlands, the <u>numerus fixus</u> has been applied in the universities only in a few subjects, mostly medical-related, and even in these subjects applications appear to be running at not more than two for every place. It is thought that most unsuccessful applicants enrol in other subjects where there is still spare capacity. In higher vocational education, however, although statistics are quite unreliable, there is thought to be excess social demand, which forces an unknown number of unsuccessful applicants onto the labour market. In Sweden, finally, demand for places in many of the open faculties has now dropped far below its maximum and excess demand is not foreseen as a problem for the system as a whole. Even in the restricted faculties, where applications in the late sixties were at the average rate of two for every place, the pressure has declined (without any increase in capacity) to near 1.7:1. In medicine, however, applications have stayed consistently high, at more than ten for every place. In summary, these examples of market economies appear to be experiencing quite different levels of social demand relative to capacity and to be adopting a variety of policies ranging from qualified response to restraint.

Unlike some market economies in Europe, Sweden, the Netherlands and the Federal Republic of Germany, all set a standard qualification for entry to university, rather than using competitive entrance examinations. By contrast, most of the centrally planned economies not only use entrance examinations as a way of controlling demand; some (for example, the German Democratic Republic) also control entry to the type of secondary school which prepares young people for university entry. Where social demand is controlled in this way, application ratios do not have the same meaning as in the Netherlands or the Federal Republic of Germany. Nevertheless, actual applications are monitored in most centrally planned countries, not only to ensure that the level is adequate to fill available places, but also in order to take some account of excess demand. In the German Democratic Republic, for example, while admission to matriculation-level senior secondary schools (EOS and BAA) is controlled, it is kept at a ratio of approximately 1.2 or 1.3 for every one university place. Despite this, in some disciplines (such as medicine and philology), the ratio of applicants to admissions is far higher. In both Poland and Hungary it is recognised that there is a substantial deficit of available places, in Hungary creating considerable "social pressure" on higher education institutions. Over the last 15 years roughly 40 per cent of those who applied to take the entrance examination have actually been admitted to higher education; again, there are marked differences between fields of study, with the toughest competition in subjects such as philosophy and arts, natural sciences, fine arts, arts and crafts, and physical education (Ivan, 1977). In Poland, even after allowing for the near 50 per cent of applicants who failed the university entrance examination, there was a deficit of places for those who passed of between 15 and 22 per cent between the years 1965 to 1975 (Kluczynski and Jozefowicz, 1977). A technique used in both countries for reducing some of the social pressure is to allow unsuccessful applicants to re-apply in succeeding years.

Although the tendency should not be overstated, it is possible to see quite strong elements of convergence in recent years between the market and the centrally planned economies in their response to the pressures on higher education of, respectively, economic needs and social demand. On the one hand, market economies which have been committed without qualification and often as a constitutional imperative to provide places for all qualified applicants, and had thus treated social demand as the sole formal criterion determining the size and shape of enrolment, have begun to restrict enrolments directly, as well as using techniques to stimulate or restrain the underlying demand. (This change should not be exaggerated: attempts in the Federal Republic of Germany to take even crude account of manpower needs have not been highly regarded and there is still an overwhelming tendency to regard the "right to education" as a basic and inalienable civil right.) Meanwhile, the centrally planned economies have moved from an overwhelming emphasis on planning in response to economic needs towards an increasing acknowledgement of the importance of social demand, which is seen as a symptom of generally rising expectations in an era of increasing private and public affluence.

So far in this chapter we have discussed the possible uses of higher education to society and to the individual. Underlying the discussion, of course, has been the question of the degree to which these various functions are, or could be made, amenable to rational planning. But the discussion has been confined to the role of higher education in its teaching capacity. It must not be forgotten that universities (and, to a lesser extent, some more specialised professional schools) are also places where research is carried out. Indeed, in many of the countries under discussion, these are the primary or even only location for all but the most immediately applicable research which may be carried out within the enterprises that need it. Even with fairly free interchange of information (which does not occur in all fields) research, or the function of creating knowledge may well be as critical for economic growth as the training of manpower. And, unlike the manpower training function, productive research, especially of a fundamental kind, seems to be much less amenable to planning. Research teams and their environments seem often to be fragile and unpredictable. Moreover, and more seriously for the planner, the productive organisation of research may well not fit easily into a rational plan for teaching. There is an obvious temptation to try to divorce research from teaching, by placing the research function in separate institutes or centres. But it is not entirely fortuitous that research is conducted in universities. In the right circumstances, research and teaching seem to be mutually reinforcing and indeed can cross-fertilize each other. There are clear dangers, of which the manpower planner may be particularly aware, in allowing research to dominate; those that affect the content of curricula will be discussed in Chapter 8. But for as long at least as research is one of the major functions undertaken by universities, the need to encourage it may very frequently inhibit the implementation of otherwise sensible manpower plans.

CHAPTER 3

Theoretical issues

The case for and against manpower planning

Higher education institutions perform a variety of social roles - they create, store and disseminate knowledge, they are important avenues of social advancement for individuals, they provide vocational preparation, they are both guardians and critics of the cultural traditions of a society and so on. However, the central task of nearly all higher education institutions is teaching. This teaching role can at its simplest be seen as an input-output system in which an input of students with certain levels and types of knowledge inter-act with teachers, books, equipment, other students etc., and is converted to an output of graduates with higher levels or different types of knowledge.

The size and structure of this input-output system can be determined either by the amount and type of inputs available to be processed or it can be determined by the desired levels and composition of the output from the system. More specifically, the provision of teaching facilities in higher education can be based upon two alternatives - and, in many ways, opposed criteria - the estimated demand for places by individual students, or the estimated demand by the economy for the qualified manpower provided by higher education. Both approaches can involve the use of statistical and econometric techniques and the collection and analysis of large amounts of quantitative data. Technical aspects of manpower planning for higher education provide the subject matter of Chapters 4, 5 and 6. Our present concern is with more general conceptual issues.

There are broadly two reasons why it might be thought desirable to plan the provision of higher education on the basis of manpower needs. The first is that higher education makes extremely heavy demands on society's resources and it is inefficient and inequitable to treat it simply as a luxury consumption good for a relatively small number of people. The second is that even in countries where higher education provision is based upon social demand a very high proportion of the students do themselves consider that it has vocational implications for them (see for example King et al. 1974). Unless appropriate jobs are likely to be available for students their social demand for higher education is itself based on a misapprehension.

However, the fact that a strong case can be made for using manpower considerations as one of the main bases for planning the provision of higher education does not necessarily mean that it is possible to do so. There are two main reasons why it might be desirable but impossible. The first is that the amount of information required and the frequent changes brought about by technological progress and social change may make it virtually impossible to assemble the data necessary in order to make useful manpower forecasts. The second, particularly prevalent in market economies, is that the nature of the economic system is such that there may be no clear relationship between the economic activity of an individual and his educational qualifications. According to this view the economic system is characterised by great flexibility and numerous possibilities of substitution between different categories of manpower.

The relationship between educational qualification and economic activity is certainly complex and differs between economic systems and even between different sectors of the same economy. The most straightforward conceptualisation, as already mentioned, is an extension of the input-output system used as the main basis for economic planning in the centrally planned economies and pioneered in the United States by Wassily Leontieff. In brief, the starting point for this system is a set of required final outputs of goods and services which are given by assumptions about consumer preferences and more general social and political priorities. The potential availability of such final goods and services is usually assumed to increase through time as a result of capital accumulation, technological progress and improvements, through education and training, in the over-all quality of the labour force. In order to provide these final goods and services a series of intermediate outputs is required. To produce a motor car of a particular type, for example, requires a known amount of steel, of plastic, of glass, of paint and so on. It also requires inputs of labour of various kinds, skilled machinists, assembly-line workers, metallurgists and, if we consider not just the making of a motor car but the organisation and marketing of motor-car production, there is also a need for administrators, sales staff, accountants and so on. Thus, if economic plans or forecasts envisage a certain output of motor cars for consumers to enjoy, they imply a particular capacity for the steel and plastics industries and also a particular level of availability of the various kinds of skilled workers required in the production and sale of motor cars.

Shortages of any of these specialists can cause bottlenecks and prevent the realisation of the planned output of cars in the same way as does a shortage of steel and plastic. Thus, economic planning, as well as ensuring appropriate production of other intermediate goods, must also ensure that there are adequate numbers of skilled workers.

Provided that young people have sufficient basic general education and facility in basic manipulative operations, many of the skills required in employment can be learned at, or close to, the place of work. However, in some categories of employment a much higher level of general education and a much more theoretically based vocational preparation is normally required if the tasks are to be performed successfully. Higher education provides this general education and theoretically based vocational preparation at considerable public expense. It is, therefore, necessary to treat the planning of higher education as an integral part of over-all economic planning, although there are a number of special problems, related in particular to the long-time horizon over which higher education decisions must be viewed.

A long-time horizon is necessary for two reasons: first, because people with high-level qualifications stay in the labour force for up to 40 years and, second, the minimum length of time for a higher education course is three to four years; a considerably longer period is needed in order to ensure that teachers, buildings, etc. are available.

The problems associated with this long-time horizon are stressed by oponents of manpower planning. They claim that, while it may be valid to view the economic system at a particular point in time as a matrix of inputs and outputs, such a view is less valid the longer the time horizon under review. Input-output coefficients change for two separate reasons. One is that technological progress changes the values of the coefficients, often in unpredictable ways. The advent, for example, of computerised control of machine tools or of banking operations can radically change the requirements for workers with particular kinds of skills. The input-output relationships are also affected by changes in the prices of the different factors of production. For example, the probability that petroleum fuel will become scarcer before the end of the present century is likely to lead to the commercial development of substitutes for the internal combustion engine. This will have considerable implications for the types of skill that are needed amongst people who are already in the labour force and those who will be entering it during the next few years.

One way out of this dilemma is through life-long education which is discussed in Chapter 9. There it will be shown that life-long education is one way of reconciling the manpower demand and social demand approaches to higher education planning.

However, another view is that the substitutability between different kinds of skills and the changing relative demands for different kinds of specialised manpower are such persuasive aspects of any growing economy that these, rather than the fixed coefficients of the input-output system, must be the starting point for the planning of higher education.

While in the centrally planned economies, it is argued that there can be no logical distinction between manpower needs and requirements - in this context both are related to specific economic, social and political goals or targets - many writers in Western Europe have drawn a distinction between _needs_, _requirements_ and _demand_ for qualified manpower.

1. The _need_ refers to the number of workers considered desirable to achieve a general policy objective such as economic growth or particular kinds of cultural development.

2. A _requirement_ refers to the number of workers technically necessary to achieve a specific objective, for example, a given level of output in the motor-car industry or a target teacher-pupil ratio. It is assumed that once economic and social targets have been set, the _requirement_ for particular categories of manpower is determined through the available techniques of production or through demographic development or something similar.

3. The _demand_ refers to the relationship between the wage rate and the _number_ of jobs for which employers are willing to hire people at that rate.

According to the critics who argue along these lines, manpower planners make a logical mistake in assuming that the _requirements_ for qualified manpower are necessarily the same as the _effective economic demand_.

Opponents of manpower planning also draw attention to the fact that the demand for skills can be met in various ways. While there may be an _optimal_ way of meeting it in the sense of providing the necessary manpower at the lowest cost, there is no _single_ way in which it _must_ be met. If employing enterprises are unable to obtain a sufficient supply of a particular kind of manpower, the earnings of people with those skills will rise and this will both attract people from other occupations and encourage others to undertake the necessary training. It is also the case that, while a particular job may be done most efficiently by someone with a particular kind of training, it can perhaps be done somewhat less effectively but at much less cost by someone with another kind of training.

The debate between those economic planners who advocate manpower forecasting for educational planning and those who sympathise with the aims but doubt its practicability can perhaps best be summarised by means of an example. Let us suppose a decision is taken to build a new general hospital in a particular urban area. Statistical records can show the probable mix of patients who will seek treatment at the hospital. It is possible, therefore, to specify how many surgeons, how many physicians, how many obstetricians, how many ward sisters, how many staff nurses, how many nursing auxiliaries, how many secretaries, how many porters and so on will be required to staff this hospital. If this is done for the whole of the health services, it shows the total national need for medically qualified people over a particular planning period. If it is done for the whole economy, it gives the total need for all kinds of qualified people.

Opponents claim that such an analysis treats the economy as a machine and not as an economic system. There are many different ways of staffing a hospital and even more of staffing a health service. If there is a bottleneck in the supply of doctors, or if the price of their services is high, many of their tasks can be performed by nurses. If secretaries are expensive, doctors and nurses find themselves doing more of their own paper work, thus having less time for their medical work which means, in turn, that more of them will apparently be "needed". Over the health services as a whole, the possibility of substitution between hospital, general practitioner and local authority welfare services is considerable. Whether a mother with a young baby is advised by a consultant paediatrician, a general practitioner or a health visitor, is in part an economic decision. It is not inevitable that an anticipated "X" thousand births will "require" so many paediatricians, so many district nurses and so on. If this is the case for the health service, it is even more true for the economy as a whole where the possibilities of substitution between different kinds of manpower are much greater.[1]

The approaches of various European countries

Chapter 2 has shown that there are fundamental differences between countries in their attitudes towards using forecasts of qualified manpower needs as the main basis for the provision of higher education. On the one hand are those which have for many years used manpower forecasts as the main criterion determining the size and orientation of their higher education systems; on the other are those which, until recently at least, have been somewhat sceptical about the desirability and the possibility of

---

[1] This example is adapted from <u>Planning Models in Education</u> by Peter Armitage and Gareth Williams, <u>Open University Press, 1976.</u>

planning higher education in accordance with qualified manpower needs. Broadly speaking, the distinction is between the centrally planned economies, on the one hand, and the market economies, on the other. In the planned economies the formation of qualified manpower is seen as a part of over-all economic and social planning. It is considered inefficient and socially undesirable to provide expensive higher education facilities for students to attend courses which do not provide them with qualifications for which there is a perceived social or economic need. It is equally wasteful if shortages of qualified manpower result in bottlenecks in economic growth. In centrally planned economies, therefore, the provision of the right quantity and quality of human capital is considered at least as important as planning the provision of physical capital.

In the market economies, on the other hand, much greater stress is laid upon the possibilities of adaptation of graduates to labour market needs after they have completed their higher education. This adaptation can come about partly through the price mechanism which will raise the relative salaries of those whose skills are scarce and lower the earnings of those in plentiful supply, and partly through the length of the waiting period during which newly-qualified graduates with different kinds of skills have to search for their first job. Hüfner et al. (1977) point out that, provided that the education and employment systems are not subjected to excessive strain, these mechanisms enable quite wide variations in the supply and demand conditions for graduates to be taken care of through labour market adjustments. Figure 3.1 shows various ways in which such adjustments can come about.

Despite the fundamental differences between these two approaches to planning the provision of higher education and despite the fundamentally different politico-economic ideologies which underlie them, it is possible to comprehend both within the same theoretical framework. The aim of this chapter and the next one is to provide such a framework. In the present chapter we consider the general theoretical basis of manpower forecasting while, in the next, we present a more formal model.

There are four fundamentally different interpretations of the role of higher education in preparing young people for the world of work.

1. During the course of their higher education, students may acquire specific knowledge and skills which they are able to use directly in subsequent employment. Thus, some learn to become mechanical engineers, others doctors, others lawyers, others managers and so on.

2. Higher education does not teach specific occupational skills but rather provides students with a general intellectual background which enables them to learn quickly the specific skills required in the job in which they eventually find themselves. According to this model it does not matter very much what is studied in higher education provided that it is intellectually challenging and stimulates the student to logical and creative thought. The objective is to acquire the general intellectual tools which will enable the new graduate to quickly learn required occupational skills and to adapt to changing requirements as his career develops.

Figure 3.1 - <u>Basic pressures working to reduce disequilibria on labour markets</u>

Disequilibria Supply and demand side	Disequilibrium 1 S D (open (or serious hidden) unemployment)	Disequilibrium 2 D S (serious labour shortage)
<u>Labour supply side</u>	Postponement of entry or re-entry to labour market, earlier retirement from the labour force, if risk of unemployment high or unattractive working conditions. Search for new job opportunities: other regions or even countries, neighbouring or even completely different professional areas; coupled with tougher competition between applicants, raising of standards. Attempts to formally restrict entry to and facilitate exit from labour markets. Willingness to accept lower hourly wages, lower salaries, lower income, less attractive work contracts, higher workload, give up fringe benefits.	Willingness to enter labour force earlier, to stay longer (within limits). Readiness to fight for better working conditions, higher pay, shorter hours (possibly negatively affecting point above). Readiness to relax labour market entry and exit provisions (inter alia, performance standards, foreigners).

Disequilibria Supply and demand side	Disequilibrium 1 S D (open (or serious hidden) unemployment)	Disequilibrium 2 D S (serious labour shortage)
Labour demand side	Attempts to lower wages, increase workloads, reduce fringe benefits. Attempts to shift from capital-intensive to labour-intensive processes and technologies if (the redundant) labour can be bought at lower price. Attempts to use relatively abundant instead of relatively scarce categories of labour. Raising of standards for applicants, lowering of beginner's earnings. Higher propensity to fire, higher selectivity in matters of promotion and advancement.	Readiness to pay higher wages, improve working conditions. Active search for additional sources of labour via lowering of standards, "importing" labour from abroad, keeping labour beyond normal retirement age. Attempts to shift to labour-saving techniques. Attempts to move production to areas (countries) with available and/or cheaper labour.

Source: Hüfner et al., 1977.

3. A third possibility is that higher education neither provides specific skills nor general intellectual training but rather is the final stage of a process of selection of young people with the basic intellectual attributes that are required in professional, administrative, scientific and technical jobs. According to this model the important aspect of higher education is neither the content nor the intellectual stimulus that it offers but rather the successive examination hurdles which eliminate a certain number of young people at each stage and orientate them towards employment that is apparently inappropriate for their innate or acquired levels of ability.

4. A fourth view is that any link between higher education and subsequent employment is fortuitous and irrelevant. According to this view, which is popular amongst some educational theorists in Western Europe, the purpose of higher education is the personal development of the individual student which can be helpful, harmful or neutral, with regard to his subsequent employment. An extreme version of this view has been put by Maslow (1973): "In the ideal college there would be no credits, no degrees and no required courses. A person would learn what he wanted to learn ... The ideal college could be a kind of educational retreat in which you could try to find yourself; find out what you like and want; what you are and are not good at."

Attitudes to the use of manpower forecasting as a basis for higher education planning are obviously strongly influenced by views about the relative validity of each of these models. The matter is complicated, however, by the fact that although there is a sharp distinction between the four views as stated, all four seem to be valid in some aspects and there are complex inter-relationships between them.

One factor not given sufficient attention in most of the literature is that "higher education" consists of many different activities. Some parts, e.g. medical education, are normally geared to fairly specific vocational training; others, e.g. courses in philosophy, are concerned mainly with improving the quality of the student's ability to reason; still others are indeed concerned with grading students according to some measure of their inherent or acquired intellectual ability while, at the same time, providing the opportunity for individual students to mature intellectually and morally. Any university normally performs all these services for its students, though the balance between them can differ very much between different institutions or different parts of the same institution.

Those countries which use forecasts of qualified manpower needs as the main basis for educational planning consider the first model to be the most appropriate. Countries which are prepared largely to accede to the "social demand" of young people tend to endorse the second model; they have a much stronger belief in the general educational functions of higher education, in providing graduates with an intellectual background that prepares them for on-the-job training in a wide range of occupations.

In practice, many of the countries which orientate their provision of full-time higher education in accordance with estimates of manpower needs are also quite likely to endorse the third model. They take the view that competition for entry to higher education is the best way of ensuring that those who are intellectually most able proceed to high-level occupations. In Poland, for example, "entry examinations remain a prerequisite for the evaluation of candidates and serve as the instrument of assessment of their ability to compete for the faculty places available" (Kluczynski and Jozefowicz, 1977).

Similarly, in Hungary, "The prescribed numbers of admission to higher education allow the most talented individuals of the age group due to continue studies to obtain access to intellectual careers" (Ivan, 1977).

Similarly, in Romania, "Everybody who has finished the lycée and who has obtained the baccalaureat has free access without distinction by sex, age, nationality, to any subject of study in higher education on the basis of an entry examination (Pestisanu et al., 1977).

It should be pointed out that provision is made in these examination procedures to ensure that all school leavers have a more or less equal chance of demonstrating their ability. In Poland, "Graduates from secondary schools in which teachers are not of a very high calibre and educational and scientific equipment is poor have, as a rule, greater difficulty in passing university examinations than their colleagues from schools better equipped both in terms of qualities of staff and facilities. In recognition of the negative effect of these differences and of the cultural and social disparities which inhibit the chances of school leavers of peasant and worker origin from competing on an equal basis for university entry, a system of social preferentiation was built into university admissions procedure (Kluczynski and Jozefowicz, 1977).

Thus, in countries which plan higher education provision mainly on the basis of manpower needs, it is nevertheless considered important to select those students who show themselves to be intellectually most competent. There is thus, implicitly at least, a selection function as well as a training function performed by the higher education system.

Conversely, in those countries which claim to provide higher education mainly on the basis of social demand, there is a growing tendency both to take manpower considerations into account for at least part of higher education and also to adopt selection procedures at the point of entry. In the Netherlands, for example, while the universities have throughout the post-1945 period used social demand as the main basis for the provision of places there has been increasing emphasis on the expansion of higher vocational education to satisfy specific manpower needs (Ritzen, 1977). Similarly, in Sweden, there has been a distinction between universities and other forms of post-secondary education. The non-university institutions, as in the Netherlands, have been much more orientated than the universities towards specific occupational training (Bergendal, 1977).

Furthermore, in Sweden, the Netherlands and the Federal Republic of Germany, there is an increasing tendency to limit the number of entrants to higher education through the use of <u>numerus clausus</u> and <u>numerus fixus</u>. Although the main reasons for <u>the imposition</u> of a <u>numerus clausus</u> are the escalating costs of higher education and the pressures on capacity it is clear that manpower considerations are an important underlying factor. In none of the countries, however, is it explicitly admitted that estimates of future manpower needs play a significant role in determining the numbers of students to be admitted in each branch of higher education. Most countries of Western Europe and North America have expressed concern about the future employment prospects of university graduates unless the rate of growth in their numbers is considerably curtailed.

Even in countries, therefore, in which there is a predisposition to plan higher education provision mainly on the basis of social demand there is growing concern about the economic implications of such decisions.

Conversely if higher education is planned mainly on the basis of qualified manpower needs this has implications for the extent to which the demand for it by individuals can be satisfied. In Hungary, for example, the proportion of admissions to applicants for full-time study in higher education declined from 66 per cent in 1960 to 56 per cent in 1970 and increasing numbers had to be diverted to part-time study in evening and correspondence courses (Ivan, 1977).

In crude terms, therefore, the situation is that countries which use social demand as the main criterion for the provision of higher education have the problems of adjustment at the point where new graduates enter the labour force. Those which aim primarily to meet qualified manpower needs have to regulate carefully the number of students admitted to various branches of higher education. The choice between them is partly a matter of ideology and partly a matter of what is most practicable in the economic and social conditions of individual countries. There can be no doubt that unemployment or underemployment of expensively educated graduates is economically inefficient and causes considerable personal distress.

In the centrally planned economies the starting point is the importance of human resources in the social and economic development of the country. "The basic task facing the higher education system - the preparation of highly qualified personnel - consists, in a planned economy, in ensuring the influx of the number of specialists needed for the reconstruction, transformation and planned economic development of the country." (Kluczynski and Jozefowicz, 1977.)

In these countries "The process of planning higher education is in general closely connected with manpower planning, and, within this, with the planning of highly qualified personnel. The determination of the number of students admitted to higher education, is based on the concrete targets of the national economic plan". (Ivan, 1977.) The situation differs somewhat from country to country but the developments since 1950 in most countries of Eastern Europe appear to have been broadly similar.

During the period up to the 1950s, although the aim was to orientate higher education systems towards the satisfaction of manpower needs, the absence of statistics and of a suitable planning framework meant that much of the planning was of an ad hoc nature and essentially short term. In Hungary for example, "The main characteristic of the initial period was that the estimation of requirements covered a medium-term plan period at the most. As transformation of the structure of school output and, through this, influence on the structure of the highly qualified workforce take a relatively long time (at least one cycle of education starting from the time of decision), the manpower plans elaborated in the initial years (around 1950) were not really medium-term calculations, just short-term ones". (Ivan, 1977.)

The reasons for this slow start are not without significance. In Hungary, "The 15 to 20 years following the end of the Second World War were characterised by a shortage of highly qualified personnel ... Because of the enormous number of vacancies, no need for a longer term assessment of demand for highly qualified personnel was felt". Furthermore, "No long term plan relating to the whole of the national economy had yet been elaborated. There was no background forecasting perspective of economic and social development against which an assessment of demand for highly qualified personnel could have been drawn up". (Ivan, 1977.) From the early 1960s onwards there began a much more systematic concern with the development of educational and high level manpower planning. Compared with the earlier plans the planning periods were much longer - 15 to 20 years - and they were directed by the Central Planning Office assisted by many sectoral working groups which undertook studies on, for example, the impact of automation on the activities of technical specialists, the impact of business mechanisation on office work and international comparisons of high level personnel.

In Poland and Romania there has been a similar gradual development of the statistical basis for manpower forecasting and the planning mechanisms for making and implementing manpower plans. "A variable which played an important role in perfecting the methods of manpower and educational planning was progress, more or less regular, in developing theoretical foundations, proper procedures and a statistical base for development planning". (Pestisanu et al., 1977.)

Similarly in Poland, "Up to the early 1960s employment planning (in Poland) was more in the nature of a passive allocation of graduates whose number and specialisation were predetermined by decisions made in earlier periods. In decision making on the allocation of resources for the development of vocational schools at various levels and their curricula, the guiding principle was, of course, the expected demand for skilled personnel, but the time horizon for analysing it was too close and the statistical and methodological bases for research were not very reliable .... In the second half of the 1960s, the first practical steps were taken towards the transition from the indicative planning stage to actual planning .... Beginning in 1964 and on the basis of the current personnel census, work started for the first time on the preparation of local skilled personnel balance sheets with proper consideration being given to suggestions made by the production and services enterprises concerned. Also in 1964 a special body called the Inter-Ministry Committee for Qualified Personnel Requirements was associated with the Planning Commission. This Committee, whose members include representatives of the ministries responsible for training (Ministry of Science, Higher Education and Technology, Ministry of Education, Ministry of Health, Ministry of Culture and Arts) and of the employer ministries, operates in specially appointed expert teams which:

1. evaluate methods of forecasting manpower requirements in particular fields of the economy and services;

2. make appropriate forecast calculations; and

3. evaluate alternative education variants and their cost.

We may say that the employment and education planning system initiated in the second half of the 1960s allowed for the feedback effect between the labour sphere and the education sphere, thus acquiring the characteristics of effective planning." (Kluczynski and Jozefowicz, 1977.)

On two points manpower planners in centrally planned economies seem to be in complete agreement. The first is that for manpower forecasts to be of any real value for planning higher education they need to be made for very long periods ahead - at least 15 or 20 years. In Romania for example "It is the long term development plan of the national economy which constitutes the basis for the calculation of qualified manpower needs". (Pestisanu et al., 1977.) In Hungary "A long term assessment of high level manpower demand is justified as the impact of education on the structure of the workforce becomes manifest only after a longer time. The yearly and medium-term plans for high-level manpower demand are of help basically to manpower management; they are of only secondary importance from the angle of education planning". (Ivan, 1977.) Similarly in Poland "Annual and five year balance sheets are, therefore, important instruments of current employment policy. They cannot provide a basis, however, for changing the number of occupational structure specialists. This possibility is provided only by long range qualified personnel balance sheets". (Kluczynski and Jozefowicz, 1977.) This discussion is further developed in Chapter 6.

The second point which emerges clearly from the experiences of the German Democratic Republic, Hungary, Poland and Romania is that manpower planning is an important part of over-all economic planning and needs to be seen as a large-scale activity requiring substantial resources and close co-operation with all sectors of the economy. This is not how manpower planning has normally been seen in the market economies of Western Europe. In the Netherlands, for example, which has some claims to be "a planner's and forecaster's paradise (and) the first of the market economies to establish machinery for systematic economic planning within the context of over-all government policy, manpower and educational planning are not a stronghold ... manpower planning exercises are not undertaken on a regular basis and tend to be ad hoc" (Ritzen, 1977).

In the Federal Republic of Germany manpower planning has consisted largely of a few individual studies (Edding 1968 based on international comparisons, KMK 1963, based on crude projections, Riese 1967 based on an input-output model) and is not an integral part of the educational planning machinery. In Sweden, there have been several serious attempts at forecasting national needs for qualified manpower of which the most recent was that of the U68 Report on higher education. However, even in Sweden, the forecasts have been fairly aggregated econometric exercises and have not involved the detailed interaction with economic planning and employing organisations that occurs in the centrally planned economies of Eastern Europe: "The calculation of manpower needs starts from a forecast of the number of gainfully employed in major economic sectors. On the basis mainly of information on occupations in the 1960 and 1965 population censuses and in the labour force surveys for 1970 the number of gainfully employed in various occupations have been extrapolated to 1980" (Bergendal, 1977). There is certainly not in Sweden anything corresponding to the regular on-going manpower planning activities of centrally planned countries.

In brief, as we might expect, where manpower planning is taken seriously, considerable resources are devoted to it; where there is more scepticism about its desirability or feasibility far less resources are devoted to it. Not surprisingly, countries which do make substantial efforts to relate higher education to manpower needs are convinced of its desirability and feasibility while those which devote fewer resources are less sure about its desirability and very doubtful about its feasibility - at least in their types of economic system.

However, in many of the countries of Western Europe which rejected manpower forecasting during the 1960s there are now fears of substantial unemployment and underemployment of higher education graduates as a result of the massive expansion of the 1960s which was initiated to fulfil social demand. In even the richest countries of the world it is coming to be considered economically wasteful and socially dangerous to ignore the relations between the education and employment systems. The focus of manpower forecasting has therefore to some extent shifted. In the early 1960s the prime concern was to provide sufficient highly educated manpower to remove possible bottlenecks to economic growth. In the mid-1970s the main concern in Western Europe is to assess the employment opportunities available for all the graduates who are likely to be produced as a result of the pressure of social demand for university places.

So far we have been concerned mainly with the possibility and the desirability of using manpower forecasts as a basis for planning the provision of higher education. The general conclusion is that while there are considerable difficulties in making reliable forecasts of qualified manpower needs, particularly in market economies but also in planned economies, it is increasingly difficult to avoid attempting to do so.

There is, however, another less frequently noted set of difficulties. A concern with high level manpower is in most countries a concern about relatively well-paid manpower. If the number of people who are permitted to obtain the qualifications that enable them to take up relatively well-paid employment is to be limited by the forecasts of manpower requirements, admission to an institution of higher education is in effect a passport to a higher standard of living than most of the community is able to enjoy. Certainly steps can be taken to ensure that chances of access to higher education are equitably distributed and do not depend for example solely upon a student's family background. But nevertheless the outcome is likely to be one in which higher education brings specially important economic advantages to those who are fortunate enough to be able to obtain it.

The obvious answer, the abolition of earnings differentials between different categories of manpower, has not been attempted as a conscious act of policy in any country.

A related problem is that manpower planning may require fairly tight control of the available supply of highly qualified manpower so that graduates are directed into those areas of employment where they are needed most, particularly during the early years of their working life. The extent to which this is acceptable is a matter of debate. Some people recommend achieving it through the use of salary differentials and monetary incentives. Another way is through systems of vocational guidance and counselling which are discussed in Chapter 7 of this book.

Finally in this chapter we must consider some of the problems which arise in translating manpower needs into required enrolments in higher education. A typical manpower forecast would give estimates of the required stock of graduates of various kinds - 5, 10, 15 and perhaps 20 years ahead. In order to derive an educational plan from such estimates the first step is to convert them into a required annual output of graduates. (Account must also be taken of those members of the labour force who will be lost each year through death and retirement.) If the forecast manpower requirements grow at a constant rate, then the output from the education system and the number of students will also have to rise at a more or less constant rate, which poses no technical problems. But if the trend of manpower needs varies, this may indicate quite sharp changes in the required number of students. A rising rate of growth of manpower needs will require a more than proportionate rate of increase in student numbers; whereas a levelling off will require a more than proportionately reduced rate of growth or possibly even a decline. A good example of such fluctuations is provided by the situation of teacher training in many countries of Western Europe. As a result of declining birthrates, the population of many Western European countries is approaching stability. The annual number of new teachers required is therefore declining sharply. This in turn leads to a much more than proportionate decline in the number of students needed in teacher training colleges. Such fluctuations create serious problems for educational planning. It is significant that in all the countries which make serious use of manpower forecasting it is emphasised that one constraint which must be observed is that the number of students enrolled in higher education should not be subject to violent fluctuations. In other words, it may be preferable to endure manpower shortages for many years rather than to expand certain branches of higher education to levels which are not maintainable in the long run.

CHAPTER 4

A formal model

So far manpower planning for higher education has been considered in very general terms. In this chapter a formal model is outlined which is intended to provide a point of departure for the detailed discussion in Chapters 5 and 6 of the techniques of manpower forecasting and of converting these forecasts into operational educational plans.

There are broadly two approaches to forecasting qualified manpower needs. One is to set targets for particular occupational categories. Most economically advanced countries have done this, with varying degrees of success, for medical doctors and school teachers (Ahamad and Blaug 1973). The second is through the use of an economic planning model in which the requirements for many kinds of highly qualified manpower emerge as part of an integrated economic plan. In both cases the link with higher education is by means of a vector of required outputs of graduates, which can be used to determine the structure of higher education and how many new entrants there will be in each branch.

In countries with extensive experience of manpower planning both approaches are normally used. For some occupations, targets are set on the basis of what are considered to be social or administrative needs, in the light of the availability of public funds to pay for them. Teachers, doctors, nurses, social workers, civil servants are obvious examples of such manpower. Other occupational groups are required, not to provide public sector services but because they produce or help to produce a saleable commodity or service.

Both types of forecasts are included in the schematic framework shown in figure 4.1. It shows a national educational planning exercise, based on manpower needs, that consists of a series of 11 steps. It is based on a simplified and aggregated manpower forecasting exercise that was recently undertaken by one of the authors in Greece.

The first step is a prediction of the level and pattern of economic activity at some future date. The main problem here is that forecasts are needed for periods of ten to twenty years - a much longer perspective than is needed for most other aspects of economic planning. For example in Poland "The long-range nature of demand for qualified manpower predetermines the way it is estimated ... the demand for specialists has to be based on a long-range concept of the development of branches and industries in the whole economy with proper consideration being given to new plants, to the expected demographic situation and to a number of other factors which will influence the volume and occupational structure of employment elements which can hardly be taken into account at the enterprise level. For this reason, the long-range demand for qualified personnel is estimated in macro-economic terms at the ministry level" (Kluczynski and Jozefowicz, 1977). Even in centrally planned economies such very long-term perspectives must rely largely on econometric forecasting techniques rather than detailed economic plans.

Figure 4.1

SCHEMATIC EXAMPLE OF MANPOWER FORECASTING EXERCISE

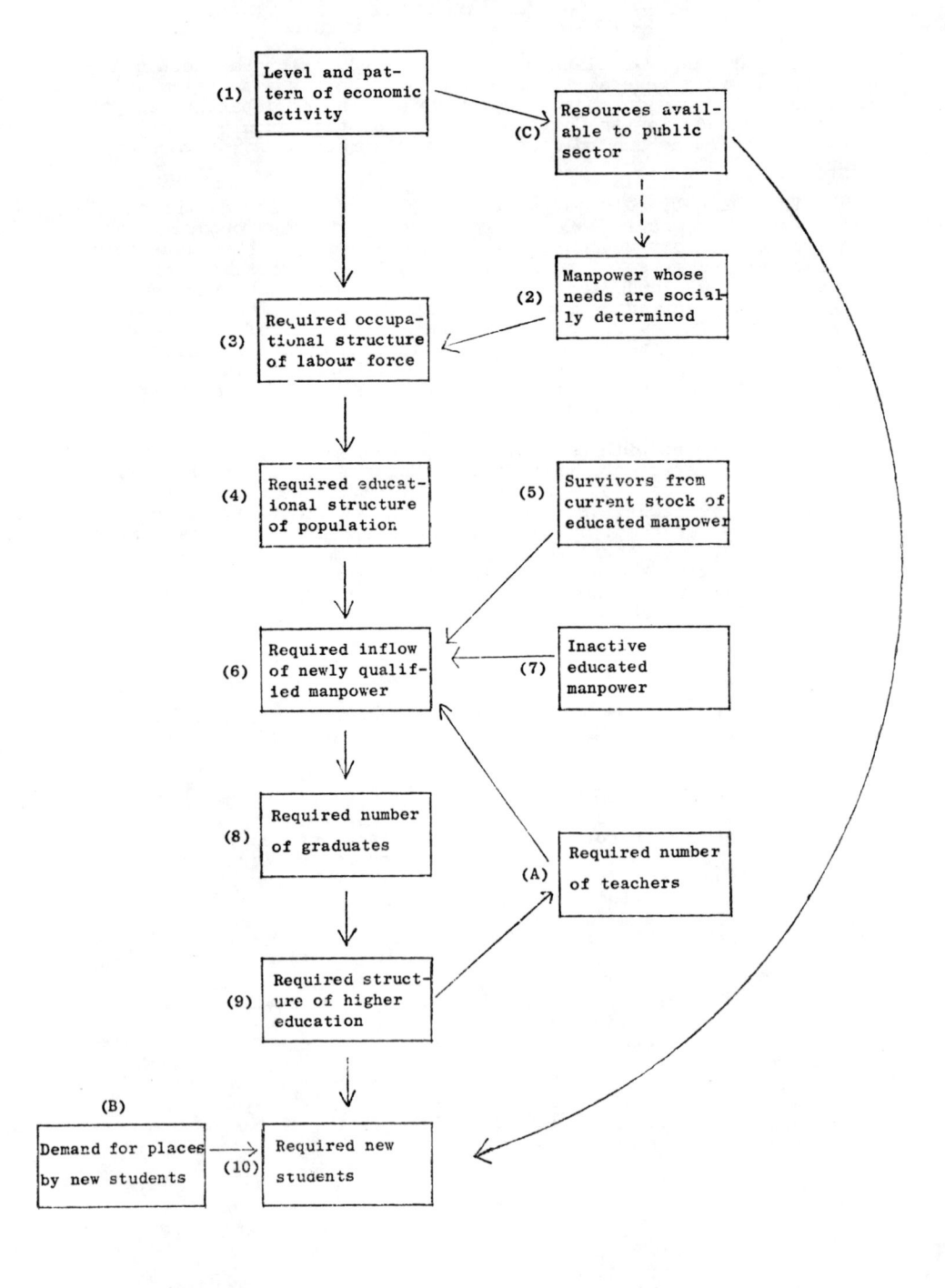

(1) Level and pattern of economic activity

(C) Resources available to public sector

(2) Manpower whose needs are socially determined

(3) Required occupational structure of labour force

(4) Required educational structure of population

(5) Survivors from current stock of educated manpower

(6) Required inflow of newly qualified manpower

(7) Inactive educated manpower

(8) Required number of graduates

(A) Required number of teachers

(9) Required structure of higher education

(B) Demand for places by new students

(10) Required new students

The fact that manpower forecasts for educational plans must be long term has caused one commentator to claim that "because of the uncertainties of technological progress if for no other reason, manpower forecasting is likely to remain an art rather than a precise science .... The art of manpower forecasting for educational planning is to find reasonable and generally acceptable bases for the establishment of targets. Clearly such an approach is in many ways not so intellectually satisfying as the attempt to establish manpower requirements linked to certain GNP growth targets: it is, however, more realistic. Public debate about the reasonableness or otherwise of the targets is as important a part of the educational planning exercise as the calculation of sophisticated forecasting coefficients" (OECD, 1967). In the light of this last comment it is interesting to note that detailed discussions amongst the various authorities involved is a central part of the manpower planning machinery in Poland. "The proposals of the ministries are discussed at meetings in which the representatives of these ministries, the management of the Planning Commission and Scientific Workers participate; then, if necessary, the proposals are corrected and approved .... On the set of problems of projecting the more important social, economic, technical factors and the main proportions of the prospective manpower structure that exert an impact on the evolution of the manpower structure up to about the year 2000, we worked up the written opinions of some 100 experts"(Kluczynski and Jozefowicz, 1977).

The second step in the manpower planning exercise consists of setting targets for those occupations for which this is considered appropriate. Independent estimates are made of the needs for the types of manpower whose level of employment is largely socially determined, such as teachers and doctors. (These forecasts are nearly but not entirely independent of economic forecasts. Although the "need" for doctors or teachers is not closely related to the level of national income, such specialists must be paid. It is unrealistic to allow estimates of "needs" or "requirements" to depart too far from the likely economic "demand", that is the number that the government sector is likely to be willing and able to pay for.) However, the main basis for forecasts of the needs for doctors, teachers and similar personnel is demographic. Requirements are calculated on the basis of formulae: so many teachers per thousand of the population aged 5 to 15, so many doctors per thousand of the population aged 0 to 5 and so on. Other public sector forecasts may be more loosely (or arbitrarily) connected to population size - for example, the target number of social workers will probably be related to estimates of the numbers of people in need of the kind of help that social workers can give. Obviously the setting of targets for particular sectors must rely heavily on the informed discussion amongst experts and political leaders which we have already described.

The third step is to derive from the general economic forecasts some estimates of the numbers of people who will be required in each occupational category in order to provide the projected output. This step is discussed in detail in Chapter 5. The only general remark to be made here is that the concept of occupation is not always an easy one to deal with.

In theory all workers are engaged in an identifiable job or occupation. Certainly for job placement and counselling activities the concept of an occupation is invaluable. Moreover, most countries now have a detailed index of occupations which have been brought together internationally as the International Standard Classification of Occupations (ISCO). Once an occupation has been defined, it then becomes possible, at least in principle, to subject it to work analysis, in order to decide on the education and training which will be necessary for satisfactory job performance. However, it is also possible to take the view that a rigid concept of occupation is unnecessary, and possibly even detrimental to educational planning. Most occupations, and certainly all of those at the higher levels, consist of a number of different tasks; these tasks can be combined in a variety of different ways, depending on the skills and abilities of people seeking to enter the occupations. Thus the occupation "secretary" - which is apparently well defined - can vary considerably depending on the ability and educational background of the people willing to undertake the job. Any attempt to define precisely the educational requirements for a secretary is likely to limit unnecessarily the range of people considered able to enter this occupation. Moreover, it may well hinder increases in the efficiency of office organisation.

Another issue of considerable practical concern is the degree of detail necessary in specifying occupations. It is clearly unrealistic to attempt to predict the numbers of employees which will be needed in very detailed occupational groups for very long periods into the future. On the other hand, the more that occupations are aggregated, the larger is the total number of individual tasks that are combined in a single category and the greater is likely to be the variety of educational backgrounds of people entering each occupational group.

Such considerations have led some observers to suggest that step 3 (the conversion of economic output targets to occupational requirements) should be eliminated altogether; the educational structure of the labour force would then be linked directly to economic activity. This seems an extreme way of dealing with a problem that is difficult but not insuperable.

At the end of steps 2 and 3 the planning team will have a vector of occupations showing the required, or acceptable, stock of men and women in each occupational category, having taken account both of economic growth perspectives and of demographic and social priorities.

Step 4 is the conversion of these occupational "needs" into requirements of various categories of educated manpower. This is done explicitly or implicitly by multiplying the vector of occupational "needs" by a matrix of coefficients showing the proportion of workers in each level and type of education. If the concern is primarily with planning higher education this matrix will, of course, focus mainly on the occupations in which most highly qualified manpower is concentrated. Decisions about the future values of these occupation/education coefficients are again a combination of trend projection, econometric analysis and judgement by experts. The techniques used in various European countries are discussed in Chapter 5.

Step 5 consists of making an estimate of the number of people from the existing stock of educated people who are likely to die or withdraw from the labour force between the base year and the target year. In step 6, the survivors from the existing stock are compared with the required numbers derived from step 4 and the differences between the corresponding elements of each vector give the required output of different qualifications from the higher education system over the planning period or periods. This output is then adjusted in step 7, by making an allowance for the (generally small) number of people who graduate and then do not enter the labour force.

Step 8 consists of phasing this required output of graduates year by year over the planning period. Probably the most important consideration here, stressed by all those countries which undertake systematic manpower planning, is to ensure that there are no unnecessary fluctuations in student numbers over the planning period. Indeed, one must also consider what is likely to happen at the end of the planning period. A rapid build up of enrolments to overcome immediate manpower shortages as quickly as possible can lead to at least a temporary oversupply shortly thereafter. During the 1960s, many developing countries of the world found themselves in this situation, owing to their anxiety to emerge from colonialism as quickly as possible by training their own people for senior positions in government, commerce and industry. In many European countries too, attempts to overcome what seemed like a chronic shortage of teachers by expanding training facilities resulted in over-capacity by the mid-1970s. (Here, it must be admitted, the problem was exacerbated by the decline in births which occurred in most European countries from the mid-1960s.)

Step 9 consists of converting the required annual number of graduates into a required number of students. This and step 10, the estimation of the required new entrants to each branch of higher education, are discussed in detail in Chapter 6. There are various ways of making such estimates; the most systematic, if appropriate data are available, is by a matrix of transition coefficients which trace the flows of students through each year of study in each branch of higher education.[1] Such models are now extensively used in UNESCO statistical activities and the model-building involved has been comprehensively described by Thorstad (forthcoming).

These ten steps constitute the essential elements of a manpower forecasting exercise, leading directly to estimates of the required number of total enrolments and of new entrants in each branch of higher education.[1] However, in order to complete the operation

---

[1] For those who like algebraic formulations the whole process has been summarised in Blaugh (1970) as follows:

The entire method is neatly summed up in the identity involving the multiplication of a scalar (1) by a row vector of fractions of GNP originating in different industries (2) by a column vector of labour-output coefficients (3) by an industry-occupation matrix (4) by an occupation matrix (5):

(footnote continued on p. 42)

there are a number of additional steps, embodying possible alternative procedures and checks on the feasibility of the projections. These are now outlined briefly.

The first has been designated (A) in figure 4.1. This is an estimate of the number of teachers in higher education which will be required for the planned number of students. Making such an estimate is a straightforward arithmetical exercise, in that the required numbers of teachers is simply the product of the numbers of students and the required teacher/student ratio. There is, of course, some arbitrariness in the concept of a teacher/student ratio; but this presents no computational difficulty in principle. There is, however, one technical problem that can cause some difficulty, particularly if rapid expansion is anticipated: namely that teachers in higher education are themselves part of the stock of highly educated manpower. Thus the required number of teachers needs to be added to the required stock. This addition will raise the required annual output, which will increase the required number of students, which will again increase the required number of teachers. In practice, with a student/teacher ratio of 10:1 a single alteration of the calculations is usually sufficient to make the necessary adjustment.

The subsidiary step shown as (B) in figure 4.1 consists of comparing the "required" number of new students with the anticipated "social" demand from secondary school leavers and others. If manpower needs require more new students, in some areas or in general, than appear likely to be available, steps must clearly be taken to stimulate the social demand. Conversely, if social demand appears likely to exceed manpower needs, steps need to be taken through counselling or economic incentives to reorientate the social demand, or to see what measures are possible to increase the employment opportunities for graduates. Such manipulation of social demand is considered in Chapter 7.

It is possible to make the comparison between projections based on social demand and those resulting from manpower needs at any stage of the model. For example the whole operation can be undertaken so as to assess the probable implications for the size and

---

(footnote continued from p. 41)

(X) $\frac{X}{X}j$ $\frac{L_j}{X_j}$ $\frac{L_k}{L_j}$ $\frac{L_i}{L_k}$ a matrix of required workers of education

(1) (2) (3) (4) (5)

in occupation   in industry, where

X = GNP

X_j = GNP originating in each industry ($j=1,\ldots,n$)

L_j = the labour force in each industry

L_k = the labour force in each occupation ($k=1,\ldots,m$)

L_i = the labour force with each level of education ($i=1,\ldots,t$)

and $\sum_{j=1}^{n} \sum_{k=1}^{m} \sum_{i=1}^{t} L_{jki}$ L.

distribution of the stock of qualified manpower if student numbers are based entirely on social demand. Many Western European countries are confronted by this question, and by the resulting problem of how to absorb into satisfactory employment all the graduates who are likely to be produced during the next decade.

Another possibility, involving a limited manpower planning operation with a much shorter time horizon, is to examine only the employment prospects of the existing stock of students, whose numbers firmly determine the outflow of graduates for the next few years. If more graduates are likely to be seeking jobs in a particular area than there will be jobs available, this is obviously a sign that further expansion should be limited or even that numbers should if possible be reduced.

Regular monitoring of the likely short-run supply and demand can result in a higher education system that is regulated rather like a thermostatically controlled central heating system. Inherent lags in the system will make it liable to some fluctuations; but it may be thought that it is better to put up with fluctuations than to create rigidities which some see as the result of tying higher education closely to longer-range manpower forecasts.

An extreme form of such an approach involves no forecasting of manpower requirements at all, but concentrates on monitoring the first employment of university graduates. (This has been done regularly for many years in Sweden, Holland, Norway and the United Kingdom.) If it becomes apparent that graduates of some subjects are finding increasing difficulty in obtaining suitable jobs, attempts can be made, if desired, to restrain social demand in these areas.

The final check that needs to be made is to compare the likely cost of the higher education programme with the resources that are expected to be available. This is shown as step (C) in figure 4.1. Clearly, it is only possible to provide a very rough check. Moreover, decisions about the share of national resources to be devoted to higher education depend in large part on political priorities; if plans for economic development are believed to depend on the availability of highly qualified manpower, then higher education will receive considerable political priority.

In this chapter we have concentrated almost entirely on the purely quantitative aspects of manpower planning - that is, on ensuring that the number of students in the various areas of study is appropriate. It is equally important, however, though much less easy to incorporate in a formal model, that the content of higher education should take into account the needs of the economy. A widespread criticism of graduates in many countries is that the knowledge and skills that they have acquired are governed more by considerations of academic respectability than by the needs of industry and commerce. Problems relating to the content of higher education are considered in Chapter 8.

CHAPTER 5

Making forecasts of qualified manpower requirements

There are many ways in which economic and educational planning can be integrated. We have already seen how the generic term "manpower forecasting" is used to describe the most frequently used planning procedure for relating economic development to educational output. However, the techniques of manpower planning are not a unique set of forecasting procedures but rather a multitude of methodologies. Among them can be found a whole range of alternative statistical procedures, as well as more intuitive methods of extrapolation and enquiry.

This chapter outlines, one by one, the main methodologies used in making forecasts of qualified manpower requirements in Europe. Although in practice each technique can be, and on occasions has been, used in isolation, it is more common for a number of different approaches to be used simultaneously. Thus the main techniques to be described should be viewed as complementary to one another rather than as alternatives. In addition, some techniques are more appropriate in some circumstances than in others. For example, extrapolation and regression techniques require reliable and exact data on manpower structure going back over a long-time period. Where such statistics are not available, alternative techniques need to be applied. Other methodologies have different informational needs.

Enquiry from employers (Delphi method)

Possibly the simplest method employed in manpower planning procedures is the survey method or enquiry from employing organisations. As its name suggests, this involves asking employers about their own intentions with respect to the employment of qualified manpower. To be useful for educational planning it is necessary to know the particular types of labour they expect to take on and the quantities and mixes of each type. Employers' forecasts are then aggregated and allowance is made for deaths and withdrawals from the labour force to give a forecast of the increase in manpower demand for the relevant target period. The method of enquiry from employers appears to be widely used, particularly as a complement to other manpower planning techniques, and seems especially common where the relationship between educational qualification and occupational task is very close. Forecasts of employment opportunities for scientific and technical manpower seem suited to this method.

Often, however, the survey approach goes beyond merely requesting details of future manpower requirements from employers. It can involve the systematic questioning of experts such as academics, researchers, planners, etc., on future manpower structures as they see it. In this way internal expectations of production and personnel can be integrated with those of external observers.

Such surveys may be undertaken by means of postal questionnaires, by interview, or by a combination of these two. Goldstein and Swerdloff (1967) suggest that "it is desirable also to interview a sample of the plants that report by mail, to find out what considerations lay behind the employers' forecasts, how carefully they were made, and whether the questions were understood by the respondents". Parnes (1962) has suggested that an interview schedule for employers might include questions on:

(a) the educational qualifications of present employees in the occupations under investigation;

(b) formal hiring requirements that the establishment currently imposes, or would like to impose, for the occupations in question;

(c) employer judgements about the general level of adequacy of existing staff in terms of job preparation;

(d) employer opinions about the "optimal" and "minimal" levels and types of preparation required for efficient job performance;

(e) employer opinions about the likely change in job content over the next 15-year period and the implications thereof for desired educational preparation.

This approach to manpower forecasting has some obvious points in its favour. Administrative difficulties are not very great, and surveys of employers' intentions are able to relay information to policy-makers and planners quite quickly. In addition, surveys of employers draw upon their detailed knowledge and awareness of the current situation, especially with respect to technological developments in progress, market and company expansion plans and other types of specialist knowledge which only those involved in an industry are likely to be aware of. It has also been suggested, perhaps cynically, that another advantage of the enquiry method is that responsibility for manpower forecasting is shared among the employers responding to the survey, leaving the organisation which co-ordinates the exercise and publishes its findings in the position of merely reporting what it has been told (Goldstein and Swerdloff 1967).

This method of forecasting also has an intuitive appeal for its simplicity. There are, however, many well-documented problems in the design and sampling procedures of any survey, and such difficulties are also present in the enquiry method of manpower forecasting. Problems that might arise include getting a proper sample of employers and/or experts, guaranteeing a high response rate, and asking appropriately meaningful questions. Other drawbacks are more formidable. The enquiry method assumes that employers do, in fact, make long-term forecasts of market shares, industrial growth and manpower requirements as a matter of course. If such forecasts are not normally made "it is very likely that they (employers) will fill out the questionnaires at least cost, that is, by guessing" (Blaug 1970). Goldstein and Swerdloff (1967) also suspect that this is a likely outcome. Moreover, even if respondents are fairly accurate in their own forecasts of manpower requirements, they cannot provide statistics for potential new enterprises not existing at the time of the survey. A further difficulty is that unless employers are specifically asked for future production levels, their assessment of manpower demands cannot be checked for consistency. Again, employers are likely to make very different assumptions about future market shares and sector growth: such differences can lead to grave difficulties when responses from all employers in a particular manufacturing sector are combined. The price of labour creates a further complication. Using the economic sense of the word demand, "unless employers are asked to forecast their requirements at various wages, the forecasts cannot be interpreted as forecasts of manpower demand" (Ahamad and Blaug 1973).

The employer enquiry method assumes that respondents are able accurately to forecast technological developments in their own sphere of manufacture. As has been suggested above one might expect employers who are intimately acquainted with their industry to be in a better position than others to predict such changes. But there are also innovations that no-one is able to foresee. Such advances may even be especially difficult to anticipate for those who are closely involved in the details of industrial production and thus, perhaps, "unable to see the wood for the trees". Specifically such employers may have a limited view of the possibilities of substituting different categories of manpower.

One knowledgeable commentator has suggested that even though such difficulties are well-known and well documented in the literature "they continue to be ignored by intrepid manpower forecasters" (Blaug 1970). Nevertheless, some of the difficulties can in fact be avoided. Some problems are simply less likely to occur in centrally planned than in market economies. Examples are non-response bias; the failure of employers to plan ahead systematically; and the problem of market shares. These differences are the result of different industrial and decision-making structures: in centrally planned economies economic forecasting may be part and parcel of normal plant management, whereas in market economies the entrepreneurial function and the competitive market structure makes the future less predictable, even when employers can be persuaded to make relatively long-term plans.

Finally, however, even if employers' assessments of future manpower requirements are somewhat less than ideal, the enquiry procedure itself may well be effective in other ways. For instance, the survey itself may serve an educational purpose by causing employers and plant managers to consider seriously their future manpower requirements, their mix of capital and labour inputs and possible technological change. In provoking such reflections, the enquiry method could well stimulate not only planning activities but also the training (and retraining) of skilled labour.

Extrapolation of historical trends

The idea of simply extrapolating historical trends in employment, has, like the employer enquiry method, a certain intuitive appeal as a method of forecasting manpower requirements. Of course, some kind of historical perspective is essential to any forecasting procedure: the current situation and possible future trends can only be properly assessed in the light of past experiences. Ultimately, however, the justification for projecting past trends into the future must be the assumption that the combination of influences which affected employment structures in the past will continue to do so, in the same way, in the future. But it is scarcely likely that the future course of any social or economic tendency will be a simple projection of past events. Economic history is full of examples of trends changing; indeed, manpower problems are most severe where a rapid departure from past experiences has taken place.

The historical approach, in its most simple form, involves the quantification of the relationship between manpower usage and output. If a fairly stable relationship seems to exist between the two, one may then project the trends identified by this exercise into the future. However, past data on trends in employment patterns are

based on the influence of both the demand for and the supply of
labour. This interaction poses problems of interpretation. The
"identification problem" is further compounded by the fact that
both output (whether aggregated nationally, by industry or per
capita), and more significantly, the means by which this output is
produced, are changing through time. Thus there is a whole network of changing and interacting influences on both supply and
demand sides of the manpower equation which create formidable problems for the interpretation of historical trends.

The first prerequisite of this type of extrapolation method,
based on historical precedent, is reliable statistics for a long
time period, in which changes in output and/or employment structure
are relatively steady or at least easy to interpret. It is also
evident that when projecting from past trends care must be taken to
eliminate periodic or random fluctuations that are identifiable as
not being part of the long-term trend. There are many problems of
detail in deciding exactly what to extrapolate and how to extrapolate it. Projections of absolute numbers, projections of proportions and projections of rates of change of numbers and of proportions all lead to very different results. Similarly, it is
often difficult to decide whether a particular trend is linear, log
linear, quadratic, sigmoid or corresponds to some other even more
complex mathematical function. Even if the basic statistics are
very good it is in practice almost impossible to make a meaningful
extrapolation without some idea of underlying cause and effect
relationships.

One variant of the extrapolation method has been called the
ILOR or Incremental Labour-Output Ratio method (Blaug 1970). In
this notation, "labour" refers to a specific occupational group and
"output" to national income or industrial group. In the 1960s,
for example, forecasts of the demand for manpower with engineering
qualifications in the Netherlands were made by using data from 1900
to 1956 to extrapolate a linear regression of the number of engineers
on national income (De Wolff 1963). In the same period the demand
for engineers in Sweden was forecast using trends in output per
engineer and the percentage of manpower employed as engineers in
different sectors of the economy (Döös 1963). Reliable time-series
data on per capita output by economic sector, occupational classification and educational qualification are necessary for this method.

International comparison

The basic premise behind this method of forecasting manpower
requirements is that different countries follow the same "world manpower growth paths", so that at the same output level they will
share a common occupational and educational structure of the labour
force. If this is in fact the case, developing countries could
learn from the experiences of other economically more developed
nations. This particular method of manpower forecasting, based as
it is on international comparison, has been termed the analogy
approach (Hollister 1964).

To be generally valid this approach needs to fulfil a set of
very restrictive conditions. As O'Donoghue (1971) outlines them:

> First, the future pattern of demand in the poorer country
> would need to correspond to that at present existing in the
> advanced area. Secondly, it would be necessary to have knowledge of, and access to, technological processes developing in

the same way. Thirdly, it would be necessary for the input combinations to be determined in the same way. Fourthly, it would be necessary to have a rate of capital accumulation with respect to income that was similar for the two economies. Finally, it would be necessary either to have no foreign trade, or that both economies should have access to the same markets for goods and services, and the same endowments of resources, so that relative prices vary in the same way in each of the economies as income increases.

Because of the strict nature of these conditions, the expectation is that direct comparisons between countries are unlikely to be valid. In fact; all international comparisons of this kind have shown a weak relationship between occupational distribution and output. While the use of data from a similar economy at an earlier point in time has an appealing ring about it, the difficulties become enormous when the method is examined in detail. Layard and Saigal (1966) calculated regression coefficients for a number of labour and educational categories in different sectors of the economy in 30 countries: no significant pattern was identified between output and occupational distribution. In 1970, an OECD study of 53 countries again found no unambiguous connection between the level of economic development and the educational structure of the labour force (OECD 1970). In an earlier exercise, Hollister (1964) reviewed the results of a number of inter-country studies and came to similar conclusions. Hollister also undertook an appraisal of the OECD-sponsored Mediterranean Regional Project and examined the usefulness of the analogy approach in four of the countries concerned in the Project (Hollister 1966). His chosen group of countries (Greece, Italy, Portugal and Spain) is fairly homogeneous; if the analogy approach is workable, one would expect them to exhibit similar characteristics in the relationship between output and the occupational and educational structure of the labour force. All four countries lie in the same geographical region, thereby being similarly placed for access to export markets and for import needs. They all have similar climates, thereby reducing inter-country differences in relation to production methods, at least in agriculture. While income levels are different, the variation is not very great. For all of these reasons one might anticipate that comparisons between these countries would be relatively fruitful. However, it appears that even these comparisons form very shaky foundations for forecasting manpower requirements.

There seems, in general, to be little support for the notion that an individual country's manpower requirements can be usefully arrived at by examining the occupational structure of another country.

Comparison with best practice (model method)

This method of estimating the future demand for manpower with specific skills is by means of a cross-section comparison between the more advanced and the less advanced firms or plants in an industry. This approach, like the international comparison one, can be thought of as "structural". It rests on the premise that within a given industry, the input mix of different types of labour - and indeed labour's relationship with capital - in the more advanced firms or plants can be used as a guide to the future pattern in less advanced firms or plants. This approach does not aid in forecasting the manpower structure of the most advanced firms or plants themselves, nor does it make allowances for the entry of new firms into the industry.

Underlying this approach is the idea of time lags between "best practice" and "normal practice" in economic enterprises. It is necessary, then, to make some estimate of the length of time lags, that is, the rate at which more advanced individual practices are adopted by a majority of enterprises. We need to make assumptions about the length of time an average enterprise will take to catch up before moving on to making estimates of the manpower required for such developments. One study in the United States of America has shown that the time lag between most and least advanced companies in the introduction of innovatory production techniques was approximately 20 years, average time lag being 8.2 years (Mansfield 1968). Such variations inevitably cause complications when attempts are made to produce manpower forecasts using this approach. There are, moreover, additional difficulties.

While at any one point in time, there will be an uneven distribution of practices within industry, each enterprise will not remain indefinitely in the same position in the hierarchy of industrial practices. Firms and plants are likely to change places in the "innovation league" as capital expenditure decisions are put into practice. Manpower developments such as changes in management personnel and educational and in-service training programmes will also have their effects on the rank order of individual practice. It is not clear, then, that the method concerned can substantially ease the inherent difficulties of manpower planning. Indeed, the approach may be more beneficial as an internal exercise by the firm or plant concerned than as a wider-ranging investigation, conducted nationally and encompassing a whole industrial sector.

Density ratios method (normative method)

This approach to manpower planning also travels under the titles of "ratio of saturation" and "manpower population ratios" methods. It is based on the ratio between a specific occupational group and a task-orientated parameter, or between one type of manpower and another. The first of these involves the estimation of the ratio between one type of manpower and, for example, a specific population parameter. This parameter could be the total labour force, the labour force of a particular industry, the entire population or a particular age group within it. The parameter chosen will depend on the manpower group under consideration. For example, forecasts of the demand for teachers will be based on the ratio of pupils to teacher, using school-age population as the population parameter.

In the second type of density ratio method, where the ratio of one type of manpower to another is considered, a forecast of one type of manpower will lead directly to a forecast of the other. This method is most often used in relation to occupational groups that can be thought of as being complementary to one another in working practice. This method of estimating future needs is widely used in the centrally planned economies of Europe. However, even when it is assumed that the demand for one type of manpower will move hand in hand with the demand for another, forecasting per se does not become any easier. At least, however, the method makes it unnecessary to calculate relative salaries, or estimate the possibilities of substitution between the two groups of workers.

Parnes - MRP approach

This is the fixed coefficients method of manpower forecasting that in the past has appeared in a variety of shapes and forms. In Western Europe the approach was pioneered by Herbert Parnes in the Mediterranean Regional Project (MRP); (see Parnes 1962). The Project itself, sponsored by the OECD, aimed to make recommendations on investment in education on the basis of defined long-term objectives for economic and social development, to assess educational requirements to meet these developments and to promote educational growth particularly in science and technical education. The countries covered by the Mediterranean Regional Project were Greece, Italy, Portugal, Spain, Turkey and Yugoslavia.

The MRP approach makes simultaneous forecasts of manpower requirements for all occupational groups and then converts these into educational requirements. The MRP method moves step by step from a target national income in a specified future year, determined by economic planning procedures, to a supply of qualified manpower necessary to meet this target. In the MRP, educational requirements were computed up to the year 1975 to meet defined economic developments; thus the project formulated detailed plans for some 15 years ahead. The comprehensive nature of the MRP exercise can be shown by quoting the objectives of the national research groups established to carry out the project:

(a) Estimate for the 15-year period 1960-75 the "required" number of graduates each year from the various levels of the educational system. For levels beyond the primary, these numbers must be broken down by broad subject matter area - at least into graduates of scientific and technical curricula and those of all other curricula, since the content as well as the costs of these two broad divisions of the educational system differ considerably.

(b) Estimate, in the light of (a), the number of teachers required in the several levels of the educational system. As in the case of students, teachers of pure and applied sciences at levels beyond the primary must be differentiated from all others.

(c) Estimate, in the light of (a) the number of additional classrooms, laboratories, school buildings, and the amount of equipment required, and plan the optimum geographical distribution of such educational facilities in the light of anticipated population distribution and the distribution of existing facilities.

(d) Assess the qualitative adequacy of existing educational programmes and make recommendations for needed improvements, including teaching methods and curriculum organisation.

(e) Assess the need for new or expanded educational and training programmes outside of the traditional educational structure, such as adult education programmes, apprenticeship - training programmes, on-the-job training, etc.

(f) Estimate the total capital and current costs of the expansion and improvement in education implied by the results of (b)-(e).

(g) Establish a "time-table" for achieving the required expansion and improvements over the 15-year period and prepare annual budgets showing total required educational expenditure in absolute figures and as percentages of gross national product. (Parnes 1962).

It can be seen from the above that the MRP exercise was all-embracing, covering as it does educational output, costs, qualitative aspects of education and alternatives to conventional educational structures. The setting up of output targets was not regarded as an integral part of the MRP exercise, since the purpose of the project was to detail the manpower and educational implications of a given target level of output. "In general, no attempt has been made to 'forecast' unconditionally the future rate of growth. What has been done is to establish, or to adopt already established targets for the growth of output per worker" (OECD 1965).

The elements involved in forecasting manpower requirements were outlined in eight stages by Parnes (1962) although the number of steps involved has been condensed by later commentators to five (O'Donoghue 1971) or four (Blaug 1970). The eight stages concerned can be summarised as follows:

(a) Analysis of the stock of manpower for the base year, classified by industrial group and occupation, and using an occupational classification that distinguishes manpower with different levels of educational qualification.

(b) Forecast of the size of the whole labour force for the target year and for the period between base year and target year - forecasts to be made at regular intervals (in the MRP this interval was five years).

(c) Estimate for each of the forecast years the size of the labour force required in each sector and branch of the economy.

(d) Distribution of employment for the forecast years among the different categories of the occupational classification used.

(e) Conversion of required numbers in each occupational category into data on required educational qualifications. A fixed relationship between occupation and education is assumed.

(f) Estimate future supply of manpower with each type of educational qualification, taking into account existing stocks, retirements, deaths, migration and output from the education system.

(g) Calculation of changes in output from educational institutions necessary for the supply of manpower to balance with requirements specified in (e).

(h) Calculation of enrolments necessary to achieve required output from the education system. Variables such as drop-out, length of courses, etc., will be included here.

In addition to these eight stages, which are based on Parnes (1962), there are two further inclusions that need to be mentioned. Stage nine would be the estimation of the numbers of teachers, technicians, equipment, buildings, etc., that are necessary to permit any change in enrolments specified in (h). Finally, the current and capital costs of meeting the educational programme need to be calculated.

The outline above of the stages of progression of the MRP exercise is necessarily simplified to some extent. In the MRP several methods were employed in forecasting manpower requirements based on output targets: (b), (c) and (d) above can be derived from any of the methods discussed in this chapter, and in fact a variety of approaches were employed to this end.

It can be seen from the above that the data requirements for the MRP approach are substantial. Even the starting point, the stock of manpower in the base year, requires a detailed breakdown of the labour force; age- and sex-specific participation rates; statistics on unemployment and underemployment; sector and branch distribution of manpower; education - occupation profiles of the labour force and distribution by sector and branch; trends in output per capita; rates of retirement, death, migration, drop-out, and so on. In fact the MRP approach has been criticised previously on the grounds of its enormous need for sophisticated data input. Ahamad and Blaug (1973) comment:

> Manpower data are required cross-classified by occupation and industry and by education and occupation and preferably for a number of time periods. Normally such data are available only in census years at decennial intervals and hence are often quite out of date. In addition, the education, occupation and industry classification systems used have changed so much from one census to the other that such data are not usually directly comparable over time. Data are also required for output and total employment by industry for a number of time periods.

Ahamad and Blaug also point out that because of the data requirements, the MRP method is expensive to apply.

In addition to the need for extensive data there are other difficulties associated with this approach to manpower planning. The assumption of a fixed occupation/education relationship may have the benefit of simplicity, but it is not necessarily realistic. It comes close to asserting that the employment of manpower is not influenced by the supply, i.e. that if the supply of a particular type of manpower changes, this will not influence the amount of manpower employed. In the short run this may be true; firms and plants may not be able quickly to substitute one type of manpower for another. In the long run, however, enterprises will find input factors more pliable and will be able to adjust input mixes to meet changing labour supply conditions (and consequently changing input price conditions). For example, enterprises may replace less skilled manpower by higher skilled labour whose numbers are in excess supply and, consequently, whose price is less than would otherwise have been the case. In early work only limited account was taken of manpower supply variations and the possibilities of substitution. In later applications of these techniques, however, sensitivity analysis has permitted greater scope for taking into account these effects.

Manpower forecasting techniques in practice

As might be expected, the use of manpower planning in a country is related to the amount of central economic planning in that country. Thus, the official status attached to, and the extent of use of the manpower planning techniques discussed in this chapter are very different in centrally planned and market economies.

In the German Democratic Republic, for example, manpower forecasting is regarded as an integral component of over-all economic planning, where planning involves target-setting and the organising of the means to achieve set targets (Sachse 1977). In the German Democratic Republic, many different methods of forecasting the demand for manpower are employed, mainly because it is recognised that no single practice is appropriate in all circumstances. The relationship between economic targets and the corresponding demand for manpower is estimated by sector and by branch of the economy. The different methods employed in forecasting future manpower requirements in the German Democratic Republic are shown in table 5.1.

In the German Democratic Republic an important constituent of all manpower planning exercises is the "requirements questionnaire" (Sachse 1977). Organisations responsible for managing the various parts of economy are required to notify forecasting authorities of their expected requirements for qualified personnel through the medium of periodic questionnaires. However, responses to these questionnaires have not, in the past, been found to be very reliable with the exception of forecasts of the demand for manpower that are typical of the economic activity concerned, e.g. teachers for schools, engineers for industry, etc. (Sachse 1977).

Substantial use is also made in the German Democratic Republic of international comparisons. It is recognised, however, that the greatest benefit derived from this type of "structural" exercise lies less in the ascertaining of absolute manpower requirements but more in the revelation of structural trends in the relationship between manpower mixes and output. Sachse (1977) acknowledges that comparisons of this nature are necessarily complicated, since differences in the socio-economic situation and variations in national education systems and qualification structures must be taken into account.

Recent work in the German Democratic Republic on specifying an analytical model involving multiple regression is of particular interest. Schaefar and Wahse (1977) have developed a model at the Central Institute for Economic Sciences to establish the relationship between the demand for qualified manpower as a dependent variable and various influential factors as independent (exogenous) variables. The model, which presupposes the availability of adequate data, is based on actual data on stocks of manpower from 33 universities and 20 college disciplines in 11 sectors of the economy from 1966 to 1972. On the basis of data on the growth of manpower stocks, approximately 70 influential factors were identified. These covered a whole range of economic, demographic and social factors.

This analytical model has been elaborated by Sachse (1977) using the following five stages:

(a) Determination of the stock of university and college graduates by discipline of graduates and sector of the economy.

(b) Specification of assumed economic, demographic and social indicators (exogenous variables).

(c) Examination of the relationship between stock of qualified manpower (broken down by subject discipline and sector of the economy) and the specified exogenous variables by means of statistical tests and politico-economic hypotheses. Rejection of assumed relationships not found to be significant on these criteria.

Table 5.1: Planning methods used in the German Democratic Republic

Designation of method	Content of method	Prerequisites for application
Correlation and regression analysis	Ascertain relationships between demand for graduates and independent variables such as labour productivity and technological progress; derive demand on basis of plans for such variables	Scientific selection of variables and relative certainty regarding their future movement
Model	Apply numbers and occupational structure of graduates typical of developed units (branches of industry, undertakings, parts of undertakings) with reliable experience to units expected to reach similar levels of development	Due regard for comparability particularly with respect to levels of technology and organisation
International comparison	Analyse graduate manpower stock and structure in comparable countries, particularly in the CMEA; take experience of developed countries into account; adjust plans to own level of development	Due allowance for difference in statistical method, and for national peculiarities
Staffing schedule method	Determine graduate manpower needs according to specialisation on basis of model staffing schedules and classified lists of comparable positions (e.g. different managerial functions requiring similar level of qualification)	Availability of model staffing schedules and classified lists of posts
Manning method	Determine by analysis the number of graduate employees needed to provide a given service (e.g. number of doctors per 10,000 population or per 100 hospital beds)	Availability of reliable statistics

Table 5.1 (cont.)

Designation of method	Content of method	Prerequisites for application
Staff normative method	Analyse the determinants of graduate employment in all the most important areas by use of correlation and regression analysis; determine the optimum relevant manning figures and use for planning at supra-enterprise level	Fairly extensive preliminary efforts to obtain pilot values that can be applied at supra-enterprise level
Extrapolation of trends	Calculate future trends in the graduate workforce under certain assumptions	Availability of statistical data covering a fairly long period, and relatively stable development conditions (rarely found in practice)
Estimates	Determine changes in graduate workforce on the basis of expert assessments	Availability of qualified planning experts with long experience

Source: Sachse (1977)

(d) Setting up a multiple regression equation into which the developments of the exogenous variables forecast outside the model are inserted.

(e) Calculation of stocks of qualified manpower required at various points over the forecasting period.

It is recognised that this model can provide only a first basis for the assessment of the future demand for qualified manpower, and that its specifications need to be supplemented by further activities. Table 5.1 shows the full range of techniques employed in the German Democratic Republic together with a summary discussion of the techniques used and the prerequisites for their application.

In Poland, as in the German Democratic Republic, the integrated nature of manpower planning and over-all economic planning is emphasised. Using data provided by successive employment censuses and information supplied by relevant ministries, specialist teams in each ministry analyse development trends in the employment of qualified personnel while giving special consideration to current manpower utilisation. A variety of methods are then employed in an attempt to forecast the future demand for manpower. This next stage is summarised by Kluczynski and Jozefowicz (1977):

On the basis of the currently distributed list of methods which can be used for determining qualified personnel requirements, together with a description of their advantages, drawbacks and the conditions of their application to specific sectors and branches of the national economy, teams at the ministries suggest the methods which they intend to use in their forecasting work. The proposals of the ministries are discussed at meetings in which the representatives of these ministries, the management of the Planning Commission and scientific workers participate; then, if necessary the proposals are corrected and approved.

The ministerial teams then prepare a forecast of qualified manpower requirements for their own areas of economic activity. These forecasts are then analysed and evaluated by the Planning Commission with the help of groups of consultants, in various social-scientific disciplines. In the final stage of work on the forecast, the number of new graduates required to achieve the target level of employment is calculated by discipline and sector of the economy. In calculating the number of new graduates required for the target year, the following are taken into account:

(a) increases in the number of jobs;

(b) anticipated loss of manpower through death or retirement;

(c) replacement of underqualified manpower.

As mentioned above, a variety of methods are employed in calculating the required number of new specialists. The particular technique(s) chosen is related to the specific conditions of a given branch of production or services. Kluczynski and Jozefowicz (1977) give examples of typical techniques used in Polish manpower planning:

(a) <u>estimation by experts</u> - commonly used in cases where it is not possible to use more objective methods; it is also used in Poland for cross-checking calculations made using other techniques. This method is used, in conjunction with others, in most branches of the economy.

(b) <u>extrapolation</u>

(c) <u>model method</u>

(d) <u>normative method</u> - in Poland this involves establishing manpower requirements on the basis of appropriate norms for the employment of qualified workers in relation to the unit of reference. Examples of use in Poland are:

- in transport - norms for servicing equipment;

- in education - norms for pupil-teacher ratios;

- in health services (hospitals) - norms for the number of doctors per 100 beds.

(e) <u>correlation and regression</u> - estimates of the future demand for qualified manpower are based on past relationships between the development of qualified manpower and factors determining the demand for experts.

(f) <u>international comparison</u> - in Poland this is treated as an auxiliary control method only.

It can be seen that in Poland, as in the German Democratic Republic, a variety of methods are employed in forecasting the demand for qualified manpower. Often more than one technique is applied to the same problem; the particular method(s) chosen reflects the data requirements of the technique, the special conditions of the economic activity concerned and the social, political and economic framework within which the activity operates. Often cross-checking takes place to ensure the consistency of forecasts. The idea of making several forecasts using different techniques which are then set alongside one another for comparative purposes, in an attempt to arrive at a set of forecasts consistent with target employment indicators, seems particularly common in the centrally planned economies of East Europe.

In Romania it is considered more and more necessary that educational planning be fully integrated with over-all economic and social planning. However, it is recognised that the need in education for long-term plans presents certain problems. Thus a distinction is made between the detailed five-year economic plans and the longer run perspectives that are used as a basis for planning the production of highly qualified manpower. The need for long-term perspectives makes accurate forecasts using a single technique impossible - rather a range of methods of estimation are used. Some aim at very accurate manpower balances for 2-3 years ahead. Others aim to give much broader indications of needs up to 20 years ahead.

The projection of long-term trends and broad international comparisons are viewed with suspicion. Preference is given to techniques that relate more specifically to the current economic and social development perspectives of Romania itself.

The starting point is a series of <u>norms</u> for each enterprise of different categories of manpower - since 1973 these norms have had legal status (see Pestisanu et al 1977). The main categories are production workers, immediate supervisors, enterprise managers, specialised professional and technical workers, other specialised workers and service workers. Each of these main groups is further subdivided; for example, "the category of <u>workers</u>, apparently homogeneous, is in fact very heterogenous. Elementary education, previously adequate for a worker, is now insufficient and even unacceptable even as the very concept of a worker has evolved considerably in recent years under the influence of technical progress" (Pestisanu et al 1977).

Once the structure of personnel of an enterprise is established various correlations are made in order to project these into the future. Examples are:

- correlation between the number of workers (of various categories) and the number of other categories of personnel;

- correlation between "workers" and technicians;

- correlation between personnel concerned with the financial aspect of the enterprise and those concerned with production.

An example of the results of such calculations in certain sectors of activity is given in table 5.2.

Table 5.2

Type of industry	For 100 workers		
	engineers	technicians	foremen
Coal industry	1.57	1.51	2.63
Oil industry	3.22	2.75	4.17
Machine building industries	2.52	4.15	1.93
Chemical industries	2.93	2.02	2.24

Source: Pestisanu, et al 1977.

Once these correlations are established the planned over-all employment of the enterprise is determined by various productivity norms.

In determining future needs the responsible ministry consults a variety of specialists in the various enterprises and these expert opinions are modified in the light of discrepancies revealed when the figures for all enterprises are aggregated and in the light of the expected impact of technical progress.

Hungarian experience in relating manpower planning to higher education has developed considerably since the establishment of its centrally planned economy. As a starting point in planning, as is usual, authorities in Hungary analyse official labour statistics to give a breakdown of the total labour force. In assessing the future demand for qualified manpower due attention is paid to the country's social and political goals.

In common with the experiences of the German Democratic Republic and Poland outlined above, a range of manpower forecasting techniques are brought to bear in Hungary on the problem of estimating future manpower requirements. The techniques used include those of extrapolation, regression, international comparison, enquiry from experts, model plan method and manpower norms (density ratios). With the objective of facilitating manpower planning and of establishing evaluation criteria for forecasts a number of functional research projects have been undertaken in Hungary. The range of subjects covered in these exercises have been summarised by Ivan (1977).

(a) On the set of problems of projecting the more important social, economic, technical factors and the main proportions of the prospective manpower structure that exert an impact on the evolution of the manpower structure up to about the year 2000, we worked up the written opinions of some 100 experts.

(b) Exploration and summing up of the relationships of prospective automation concepts connected with manpower.

(c) A retrospective analysis of the process of transformation of the manpower structure in the past 50 years.

(d) Comparative study of international trends in the transformation of manpower structure.

(e) In regard to the number and composition of the workforce employed in research and development, an independent calculation and analysis with a view to orienting the expected number of highly qualified specialists.

(f) Elaboration of a system of job requirements and changes in the content of the more important jobs.

(g) Impact of scientific and technological progress on the requirements set for technical specialists.

(h) Opportunities for young and adult workers to be promoted to social positions at the place of work.

(i) Analysis of the relationships between manpower demand and the open nature of society. In this framework we compared our calculations with the manpower structure extrapolated from the process of restratification which has taken place in the past 30 years.

Because of the socio-political framework within which the higher education systems of centrally planned economies operate, the close liaison between manpower planning, general economic planning and educational developments is only to be expected. Such rigid relationships are not to be found however in market economies. Whilst manpower forecasting activities are in evidence in countries like the Federal Republic of Germany, the Netherlands and Sweden such studies are often undertaken for their information value rather than as an aid to planning the number of places in higher education. Traditionally, in most areas of study in Western Europe, social demand has been the basis of most quantitative planning of higher education. There are always exceptions, particularly in medicine, teacher education and some branches of science and technology, but in the main the measurement of social demand has been the primary activity of higher education planning. More recently, with the more widespread use of numerus clausus by public authorities, some attempt has been made on occasions to restrict student numbers in certain subject areas where labour market conditions have shown evidence of graduate employment difficulties. But more often it is left to the market to resolve difficulties of over- and undersupply of qualified manpower through the medium of substitution, salary differentials and unemployment, coupled with counselling and media publicity.

In market economies, whilst it is recognised that the development of qualified manpower is an important objective of higher education, great store is placed on other tasks such as individual development, socialisation and the fostering of academic interests. Recent financial crises in the West and the rapid escalation of the costs of higher education have led to many commentators urging a change of emphasis in planning procedures and specifically that manpower forecasting should assume greater importance in planning higher education. However, given the weak link in market economies between subject of study and subsequent employment of graduates, these claims have gone largely unheeded. In parliamentary discussion on numerus fixus in the Netherlands it was agreed that manpower forecasts were too unreliable as a basis for policy when assessing the future labour market position of graduates (Ritzen 1977). Discussions in other countries of Western Europe have followed a similar course.

In the Netherlands higher vocational schools have the right to refuse students in excess of their specified admission capacity. Although labour market conditions do not directly determine this capacity it would appear that the graduate employment situation is an important indirect influence. Universities in the Netherlands can apply for specific areas of study to be governed by numerus fixus regulations, and while again in principle labour market conditions do not influence the limitations on admissions, evidence suggests that the labour market is often of importance in this. "The connection between disciplines with numeri fixi, the actual admission capacity and labour market projections need not come as a surprise" (Ritzen 1977). In spite of these mechanisms to relate employment prospects and graduate output more directly, occupational remuneration, substitution possibilities and unemployment remain the most important adjustment devices. Although the Central Planning Office in the Netherlands originally made important contributions to educational and manpower forecasting, few advances have been made in recent years. Manpower and educational planning are not a central feature of Dutch planning, and in fact little attention has been paid to education within economic planning models in the Netherlands. In recent years, several forecasts of student flows have been published. The Ministry of Education has recently produced forecasts of enrolment in university education (the WORSA) and in higher vocational education (the RHOBOS) up to 1990. (The RHOBOS is not yet complete.) Details of these forecasts are given in Chapter 6. Given the Dutch emphais on planning on the basis of social demand, greater importance is naturally attached to estimates of future student flows than to those that attempt to estimate future manpower requirements. Ritzen (1977) makes the point that the crucial question in this latter type of exercise should be to find out the number of graduates who can be absorbed by the labour market at specific pay rates. It is more usual, however, for estimates of manpower requirements to concern themselves only with the number of graduates demanded on the labour market, omitting the question of price.

In any event, there have been three types of study in the Netherlands to ascertain the demand for qualified manpower. These are:

(a) Studies based on the development of the economy as a whole, or on particular sectors of it. In these, a functional relationship between the demand for labour with different educational qualifications and national product (possibly disaggregated by sector) is assumed. The work of den Hartog and Thoolen (1971) and the RABAK study (1975) are of this kind.

(b) Subjective estimates of demand based on the views of specialists in the field or surveys carried out among graduates. This example of the "Delphi technique" has been used to assess the future for psychologists by Krijnen (1976) and for physicists by de Laat (1975).

(c) Normative estimates of the demand for qualified manpower based on the relationship between one type of manpower and a particular population parameter. The work of Poorter (1977) on the demand for medical doctors falls into this category.

A variety of forecasting techniques were employed in the RABAK study (1975). In order to assess the over-all demand for university graduates, this study first analysed the historical relationship between income and the number of employed university graduates and then undertook extrapolations of labour productivity. Both exercises were undertaken for the total demand for university graduates and for demand by discipline of study. Krijnen (1976) consulted 38 experts when using the Delphi method to estimate the future demand for psychologists. These experts had substantial experience of a variety of sectors of the economy. During extensive interviews, the subject of future demand was dealt with both in terms of a quantitative forecast and qualitative aspects of employment. De Laat (1975) also used this division when forecasting the demand for physicists in 32 different sectors of the economy on the basis of interviews with 30 experts.

The Federal Republic of Germany shares the emphasis which the Netherlands places on the regulatory mechanisms of the labour market in education planning. Here, political and economic intervention takes place where market imperfections are apparent or where normal market mechanisms cannot function. It is usually in this restricted sense of decisions about the working conditions of markets that the terms "planning" and "forecasting" are understood in the Federal Republic of Germany. As we have seen this concept of planning and forecasting contrasts sharply with the notion of planning in the centrally planned economies of socialist Eastern Europe.

One of the problems which would face any possible manpower planning approach to higher education in the Federal Republic of Germany is the nature of its policy-making and implementing institutions. The decentralised nature of government and of educational responsibilities in the Federal Republic of Germany would inevitably cause difficulties. Under the constitution, education in its entirety is placed under state supervision. However, the *exercise of state responsibilities falls within the jurisdiction of the Länder. "This arrangement led - and still leads - to a number of co-ordination problems" (Hüfner et al 1977). Under this federal arrangement it is difficult to see how national manpower forecasting, with a commitment to implementation, could function. It is not surprising, then, to find that the relationship between higher education and manpower planning is a loose one, with the Federal Republic of Germany having very little recent experience of the techniques of manpower planning.

The first detailed application of the manpower forecasting approach in the Federal Republic was published in 1967. This study was undertaken at the request of the Science Council by Riese (1967). On publication it met with less than enthusiasm, a reaction that is interpreted by Hüfner et al (1977) as indicating a movement from

the accepted pre-1967 link between education and economic growth
to the post-1967 policy of educational expansion for its own sake -
"if necessary, against the principles of economic rationality"
(Hüfner et al 1977). Riese (1967) emphasised in his work that the
approach he had adopted, and the model of the demand for graduate
manpower he developed, was determined not only by the methodological
premises of the manpower approach, but also by the limited amount of
statistical material available at the time. Riese assumed an overall annual GNP growth rate of 4 per cent until 1981, disaggregating
this growth among 45 sectors of the economy. The labour force in
these sectors was subdivided into 55 occupational groups and the
university graduates of these occupational groups were assigned to
67 fields of study. Riese assumed the continuance of the structural changes that had taken place in these economic sectors since
1950 and proceeded to analyse the relationship between GNP growth
and the demand for highly qualified manpower. However, his findings, which pointed to limiting the expansion of academic higher
education so as to improve the quality of the educational system
itself, were not in sympathy with the dominating theme of the late
1960s - the active stimulation of the social demand for education.
This accounts for the muted reception of his work in the Federal
Republic of Germany.

In Sweden the 1955 University Commission for planning higher
education in the 1960s used a manpower planning approach for some
of its work. The future demand for such manpower categories as
civil engineers, physicians, dentists, pharmacists, agronomists,
foresters, veterinary surgeons, economists, lawyers, public administrators, priests and teachers were all estimated by the Commission.
Calculations were also made of the outflow from the school system,
expected future enrolment in higher education and the number of new
graduates.

Subsequently, however, developments exceeded these forecasts
both in the demand of the economy for new graduates and in the
demand for higher education by young people.

Thirteen years later, quantitative aspects of educational
planning were again dealt with - this time by the 1968 "U68"
Educational Commission. At the outset this Commission stated the
collective belief that although forecasts of the future demand for
qualified manpower can never be the only criterion of planning higher
education in Sweden, such a consideration is one of the essential
elements to be taken into account. A basic premise of the Commission
was that the goal of educational planning was <u>not</u> to match the outflow
from the education system perfectly with the demands of the economy.
This is regarded as being too rigid a view of educational planning.
Such a view, however, did not preclude making forecasts of the relationship between specific educational programmes and the relevant sector of the economy. It was forcibly argued by the U68 Commission that
in the case of long, highly specialised training programmes with high
costs, capacity should be closely related to manpower requirements.

The main concept of forecasting that underlies current planning
practices in Sweden is straightforward: to calculate, in comparable
terms, the estimated outflow from the educational system and the
estimated manpower requirements of the economy. Indeed, "all
computations on future demand for higher education, on the flow
through the educational system, and on the number of graduates, have
more the character of calculation exercises than of forecasts"
Bergendal (1977).

The calculation of estimated manpower requirements in the U68 report started from a forecast of the numbers employed in the main sectors of the economy. On the basis of information on occupational structure in the 1960 and 1965 population censuses and in the labour force survey of 1970 the numbers employed in various occupational groups were extrapolated to 1980. Calculations were then made of the total need for new recruitment in different occupations and the proportion of new recruits to be drawn from the education system, over five-year periods. The percentage of manpower with various educational backgrounds in total new recruitment were estimated on the basis of data from the 1960 population census, from follow-up surveys of new graduates and on the judgement of a group of experts. However, it was recognised that calculations in relation to student flows are subject to considerable uncertainty. This has also been found to be the case with forecasts of the future demand for qualified manpower. Analysis of the Swedish situation has shown that general economic development is by far the most powerful source of uncertainty (Bergendal 1977). As with other market economies, it is recognised in Sweden that manpower forecasts are just one of a series of factors that have to be taken into account by political decision makers.

There are clearly numerous techniques that can help to calculate the future demand for qualified manpower. The extent and frequency with which they are used is very largely determined by the socio-political framework within which planning takes place. Thus, in countries where widespread state intervention in economic planning activities is common, the commitment to integrating manpower planning and higher education is high. Where the regulatory mechanisms of the labour market, such as substitution, salary differentials and unemployment, are less tempered by governmental activity, countries have a relatively weak commitment to manpower planning as an organ of control. We have seen above the contrast between centrally planned and market economies in their commitment to manpower forecasting. The experiences of centrally planned economies such as the German Democratic Republic, Hungary, Poland and Romania in using manpower planning techniques are naturally much more extensive than those of market economies. Although countries such as the Federal Republic of Germany, the Netherlands and Sweden have all recently completed work on the future demand for qualified manpower, the main planning criterion is still a commitment to social demand; thus these studies are often not of official status, and little attempt is made to gear places in higher education directly to the demand for graduates. (As we shall see in Chapter 7, there are, however, ways of using market mechanisms such as information to influence student flows.) The widespread use of a whole spectrum of techniques in the centrally planned economies, and to a lesser extent in Western Europe has shown that no single manpower planning technique is suitable or possible for all circumstances. Often, then, more than one technique is applied to the same economic sector or occupational group to ensure consistency or to check on accuracy before any manpower plan can be implemented.

Chapter 7 deals with the process of implementing manpower based on higher education plans; we consider first, in Chapter 6, the ways in which forecasts of manpower needs are converted into education plans.

CHAPTER 6

Converting manpower forecasts to educational plans

This chapter is concerned mainly with that part of the planning exercise which converts a matrix of manpower requirements into an operational plan for higher education. It can be summarised as a series of discrete steps. In practice not all these steps are essential for all countries.

The first step is to forecast the numbers of survivors from the existing stock of qualified manpower. This involves the forecasting of mortality, retirement and mobility rates. Mortality rates are fairly easy to predict: most developed countries now have data on age- and sex-specific mortality rates that can be used to forecast the loss through death of highly qualified manpower. Retirement from the labour force in most countries is an administratively determined function of age. Although there may be more or less flexibility in different countries in individual cases, and although some allowance needs to be made for early retirement because of ill-health and similar reasons, in general the estimation of retirement rates does not present much difficulty. However, labour force mobility, both geographical and occupational, presents a more difficult set of problems. Where occupational movements occur in the normal course of career development, i.e. in promotion from one grade to the next, there is in principle no serious problem, especially in planned economies. In general, the known demographic qualification structure of the labour force provides a reasonable basis on which to work. However, occupational mobility which occurs as a result of economic growth or social change is a more difficult matter. The basic problem is that such occupational movements are the result of supply and demand interactions. Their prediction is beset with all the problems of forecasting manpower requirements that have been previously discussed. The forecaster is often forced to rely on past experience and comparison with other industries or other countries.

The next step is to add to the survivors from the existing manpower stock those students who are already in the higher education system and who will therefore emerge during the early years of the planning period. Countries which have previously used manpower forecasts to plan their higher education system will already have determined their student numbers in accordance with earlier plans. In countries that are beginning to develop manpower planning techniques, however, there will be a transition period during which account has to be taken of previously, if externally, determined student numbers. Even in countries which have been planning their qualified manpower supply for a number of years, all forecasts will not always prove to be completely correct: there is a constant revision of plans, so that student numbers which were geared to previous best estimates of manpower needs may not be ideal in the light of more recent projections. Nevertheless, the fact that students are already orientated towards a particular type of career

The next step is to compare the matrix of manpower requirements with the anticipated size and distribution of survivors from the existing manpower stock, plus those already in the educational pipeline. The differences between the two will indicate what adjustments need to be made to the output from each of the main branches of the education system.

The next steps can perhaps best be illustrated by an example from Romania given by Pestisanu, et al (1977).

As described above the qualified manpower that must be trained includes not only additional manpower to meet economic growth targets but also those who are necessary to replace deaths and other withdrawals from the labour force.

The following formula is used:

$$N_{pr} = (N_1 - N) + N \cdot \frac{p}{100}$$

where:

N_{pr} - the number of manpower desired

N - amount of manpower available at the beginning of the year

N_1 - amount of manpower at the end of the year

p - annual percentage withdrawals from the labour force

In order to prepare the educational plan, one must estimate the likely output resulting from existing enrolments and compare this with estimated future needs (N_{pr}, above). This is the manpower balance for each specialisation (see table 6.1).

Table 6.1

BALANCE OF ONE SPECIALISATION:
CIVIL AND INDUSTRIAL CONSTRUCTION ENGINEERING

– (Level: higher – Length of studies: 5 years) –

	1975	1976	1977	1978	1979	1980	1981	1982	1983	1984	1985
Specialists needed at the end of the year	1 800	1 980	2 160	2 340	2 520	2 700	2 900	3 100	3 300	3 500	3 700
Specialists foreseen at the beginning of the year	1 600	1 624	1 667	1 709	1 759	1 797	1 854	2 900	3 100	3 300	3 500
Annual drop-out (3.5 per cent)	56	57	58	60	62	63	65	101	109	116	123
Remaining specialists	1 544	1 567	1 609	1 649	1 687	1 734	1 789	2 799	2 991	3 184	3 377
Graduates foreseen:											
– current	80	100	100	110	110	120	–	–	–	–	–
– to be trained	–	–	–	–	–	–	1 111	301	309	316	323
Specialists foreseen at the end of the year	1 624	1 667	1 709	1 759	1 797	1 854	2 900	3 100	3 300	3 500	3 700
Deficit or excess	-176	-313	-451	-581	-723	-846	–	–	–	–	–

Source: Pestisanu et al, Table XXIV.

The authors comment: "The balance shown in Table 6.1 has been established with the aim of arriving at the level of enrolments necessary to meet fully the estimated needs for this category of specialised manpower from 1981 onwards. (This is the first year in which decisions taken in 1976 can affect new entrants to the labour force.) Withdrawals from the labour force are considered to amount to 3.5 per cent of existing stock each year". The table also indicates the number of graduates who can be expected between 1976 and 1980 as a result of existing enrolments; in order to arrive at these figures for graduations, it is necessary to take into account student wastage which is illustrated in Table 6.2.

Table 6.2: Wastage rates during studies

	Duration in years	I	II	III	IV	V	Total length of studies
Full time education							
Technical education (engineers)	5	6	5	3	1		15
Technical education (undergraduate engineers)	3	6	4	-	-		10
Agricultural	5(4)	5	4	2	1		12
Economics	4	5	3	2	-		10
Medicine	6	5	2	2	1	1	11
Pedagogy	5(3)	5	3	2	1		11
Fine arts	4	5	2	1	-		8

Source: Pestisanu, et al, table XXV.

For the sake of simplicity, a coefficient K is estimated, to convert the number of required graduates into a number of required new entrants five years earlier:

$$k = \frac{100}{100-p}$$

where p = the percentage of students failing to complete the course

Table 6.3 shows how K is calculated for various wastage rates.

In the case of technical education for engineers, table 6.2 showed that the total wastage is 15 per cent. By referring to table 6.3 we find the appropriate coefficient K = 1.1788. Thus, the number of new enrolments in the relevant faculties which would

Table 6.3

Wastage rates during studies	Transformation coefficient $(\frac{100}{100-p})$
1	1.0100
2	1.0204
3	1.0309
4	1.0417
5	1.0526
6	1.0638
7	1.0754
8	1.0869
9	1.0989
10	1.1111
11	1.1236
12	1.1363
13	1.1494
14	1.1630
15	1.1788
16	1.1905
17	1.2048
18	1.2195
19	1.2345
20	1.2500

Source: Pestisanu, et al, table XXVI.

be required during each year of the period 1976 to 1981, to meet the manpower needs estimated in table 6.1 would be as follows:

Table 6.4: Enrolments required to meet estimated need for new manpower, 1981-85: civil and industrial construction engineers

In 1976-77	1 111 x 1.1788 = 1 310 students
In 1977-78	301 x 1.1788 = 355 "
In 1978-79	309 x 1.1788 = 365 "
In 1979-80	316 x 1.1788 = 370 "
In 1980-81	323 x 1.1788 = 380 "

Source: Pestisanu, et al, p. 55.

From these calculations, it is apparent that, if one wished to satisfy estimated manpower needs in this particular specialisation fully by 1981, it would be necessary in 1976 to enrol 1,310 students - which is about 9.3 times the number enrolled in 1975. Subsequently it would be necessary to admit about 350-380. Such a massive increase in enrolments for one year only is neither practical nor economic; indeed, it is clearly unrealistic. Clearly the basic hypothesis underlying table 6.1 is not realisable; for it ignores the principle of educational planning that enrolments should expand at an even rate avoiding sharp rises and falls. The next problem, therefore, is to examine what rate of increase of enrolments is the most practicable.

It appears that, with the exception of 1981, an output of 320 graduates per year would be sufficient to meet the annual needs of the economy. This corresponds to 375 new enrolments each year. The enormous increase for 1981 which was proposed in table 6.1 resulted from the attempt to meet the whole of the accumulated deficit of qualified manpower in a single year. However, the new assumption of an annual first enrolment of 375 students per year would result in a gradual diminution of the deficit in the years up to 1985, as is indicated in table 6.5. Nevertheless, the deficit in 1985 would still be considerable, amounting to more than two years' production of new graduates.

Table 6.5: Modified balance

	1981	1982	1983	1984	1985
Specialists needed at the end of year	2 900	3 100	3 300	3 500	3 700
Specialists foreseen at the beginning of year	1 854	2 109	2 355	2 593	2 822
Annual wastage (3.5 per cent)	65	74	82	91	99
Remaining specialists	1 789	2 035	2 273	2 502	2 723
Graduates foreseen	320	320	320	320	320
Specialists foreseen at the end of year	2 109	2 355	2 593	2 822	3 043
Deficit or excess	- 791	- 745	- 707	- 678	- 657

Source: Pestisanu, et al, table XXVII.

Moreover, if one is to assess the proposed target output of 320 per year, it is desirable to make a further rough projection until 1990. An example of such an extended balance is given in table 6.6.

Table 6.6: Balance of year 1990

	1985	1986	1987	1988	1989	1990
Specialists needed at end of year	3 700	3 900	4 100	4 300	4 500	4 700
Specialists foreseen at the beginning of year	2 822	3 043	3 257	3 463	3 662	3 854
Annual wastage (3.5 per cent)	99	106	114	121	128	135
Remaining specialists	2 723	2 937	3 143	3 342	3 534	3 719
Graduates foreseen	320	320	320	320	320	320
Specialists foreseen at the end of year	3 043	3 257	3 463	3 662	3 854	4 039
Deficit or excess	- 657	- 643	- 637	- 638	- 646	- 661

Source: Pestisanu, et al, table XXVII.

According to this projection, the accumulated deficit would begin to increase again in 1988. In other words, the new assumption for enrolments is still not satisfactory, and it is necessary to increase enrolments still further. It can be shown that an annual enrolment of 470 new students, giving an output of 400 engineers per year, would gradually reduce the deficit until it disappeared in 1990. Table 6.7 indicates the final calculation which would show the total student population required each year to meet manpower needs in this sector fully by 1990.

Even though much of the work on manpower balances is in one sense mechanical, as this example has shown, it is clear that a considerable degree of judgement is necessary to assess which path of development is likely to be economically and socially practicable. The main purpose of the balances is to give a rigorous analytical framework within which such judgements can be exercised. For example, there are other reasons why the implications of a proposed path of educational development may be unrealistic. One possibility is that the age groups whose enrolment in higher education is being planned may not be large enough to supply the total needs of the labour force. The resource implications could also be a deterrent to putting the plan into operation. In either of these cases the required growth in enrolments and graduations may have to be adjusted, and special priorities for educational growth may have to be designated. It must be remembered too that in-service training and education by correspondence offer alternatives to full-time study as a means of achieving qualified manpower targets.

Table 6.7: Final calculation of training for "civil and industrial construction engineering"

Academic year	Study years					Total No. of students	Number of graduates foreseen
	I	II	III	IV	V		
1975-76	140	120	114	101	100	575	100
1976-77	470	132	114	111	100	927	100
1977-78	470	442	125	111	110	1 258	110
1978-79	470	442	420	121	110	1 563	110
1979-80	470	442	420	407	120	1 859	120
1980-81	470	442	420	407	403	2 142	400
1981-82	470	442	420	407	403	2 142	400
1982-83	470	442	420	407	403	2 142	400
1983-84	470	442	420	407	403	2 142	400
1984-85	470	442	420	407	403	2 142	400
1985-86	470	442	420	407	403	2 142	400

Source: Pestisanu, et al, table XXIX.

Iván (1977), commenting on the relations between manpower planning and higher education in Hungary, points out two constraints that may inhibit putting educational plans into operation. First, it may be the case that in the short term a general lack of capacity or a shortage of the necessary investment funds will prevent the development of the education system in response to manpower requirements. However, in the longer term the necessary adjustments can be made. Iván's second point is perhaps more significant. In all forecasts of this kind, some margin of error needs to be taken into account. Hence, if the discrepancy between manpower requirements and educational output is not large, it is sensible to leave the educational system as it is. In other words, allowance is made for the fact that, in the Hungarian situation at least, the system is flexible enough to permit some variations. However, aside from these qualifications it is a general principle in Hungary that if the demand for highly qualified manpower differs from the educational output expected, the education system will be manipulated to make good the difference (Iván, 1977).

In Hungary, once manpower targets have been formulated, arrangements are made to translate them into an educational plan. As in Romania, balance sheets are drawn up of the demand for and supply of highly qualified manpower. Iván outlines the calculations as follows:

$$E_d = (D - B_{wf}) + Dc_h \pm M_b$$

where E_d = educational demand in a given period

D = demand

B_{wf} = base workforce

Dc_h = natural decrease (covering retirement and mobility)

M_b = mobility balance

In the German Democratic Republic, again within a framework of balancing manpower requirements and flows from the education system, a check is made, once the calculations are complete, to see to what extent the demands for graduate manpower can be met from educational institutions. Allowance is made for employees gaining qualifications through correspondence courses, for occupational mobility, for the secondment of workers to full-time study and, of course, for natural losses from the labour force. Table 6.8 shows the framework of the calculations that are undertaken in the GDR. Planning activities in the GDR are very much concerned with the setting and meeting of specified targets:

> ... in accordance with our socialist views and our experience, planning forms a single unit comprising target-setting and the means of attaining those targets. This is of very special significance for manpower planning and the development of graduate manpower, since we are dealing with human beings who have a right to work and occupational advancement (Sachse 1977).

In Sweden the calculations of manpower needs in the U68 report started from a forecast of the numbers employed in the major economic sectors up to 1980. The extrapolation of labour force information from censuses and surveys provided the basis for these figures. Calculations were then made of the total need for new recruitment in different occupations over five-year periods to 1980, and of that part of the new recruitment that was expected to be met from the educational system. Figure 6.1 shows the principles of these calculations.

Figure 6.1

PRINCIPLES FOR THE CALCULATION OF THE NEED
FOR NEW RECRUITMENT IN AN OCCUPATION BETWEEN 1970 AND 1975 (SWEDEN)

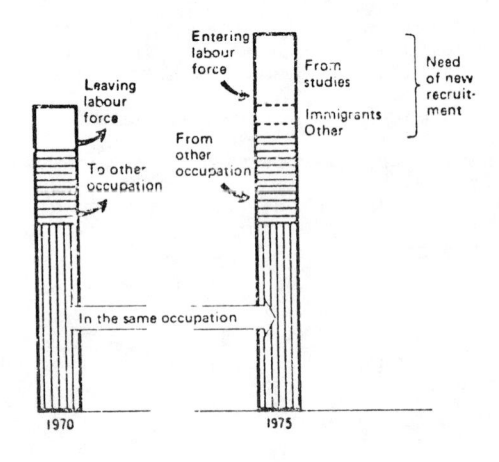

Source: Bergendal (1977) Figure 2:19.

Table 6.8: Planning section on qualification structure and demand for training (GDR)

1	2	3	4	5	6	7	8	9
		Losses		Additions total 1976-80	Components of column 5			
Stock as at 31 Dec. 1975	Stock required as at 31 Dec. 1980	Total	Owing to natural or social causes		Graduates from direct studies or apprentices completing their apprenticeship	Graduates from correspondence evening courses or adult education	Total addition	Possible stock as at 31 Dec. 1980

Qualification structure

Manual and non-manual workers
of whom:
  women
  university personnel
  college personnel
Senior craftsmen
Skilled workers
of whom:
  women workers with only partial or no training

Source: Sachse (1977), figure 4.

It can be seen that account is taken in these estimates of the stock of labour, occupational mobility, losses from the labour force and additions to it. Among those entering the labour force are the output from the educational system, immigrants and "other". The question of migration is significant. One method by which an individual country might satisfy some of its needs for qualified (or unqualified) manpower is of course to import it from other countries. Much will depend on the specific social, political and economic circumstances of the country concerned, but, in theory at least, the importation of skills from abroad is one way to satisfy a forecast of excess demand. The inclusion by Sweden of immigration as an input should be taken as an acknowledgement of what is likely to happen, rather than as a policy decision to encourage the importation of skilled labour. Amongst others, Third World countries have often used the manpower resources of the developed world as a positive measure to aid their own economic development. Such a use of migration (often on a temporary basis) can remove the problems of time-lags in the production of skilled labour; the resource implications are not severe; and qualified manpower from overseas can often be used in training indigenous labour. Thus, if immigration is available as a policy option, account should be taken of it in formulating manpower plans. In this way, countries can ease pressure on educational capacity, reduce time-lags and lessen the burden of the costs of rapid educational expansion.

The example of converting a manpower forecast to an educational plan which is given in this chapter used a time-span of 15 years; this length of time is by no means immutable. The MRP exercise, as we saw in Chapter 5, attempted 15-year forecasts. Parnes (1962), in common with other commentators, recommended that forecasts of manpower requirements should cover at least 10 years, and preferably 15 or 20 if they are to be useful in educational planning. Longer forecasts involve predicting the birth rate, adding a further complication to the manpower planner's computations. "It should be noted that ... a 15-year forecast is based upon numbers of persons already born and is not subject to errors caused by changes in the birth rate" (Parnes 1962). Parnes and others acknowledge that in forecasting so far into the future there can be little expectation of accuracy and little detail in forecasts, but of course "there is also a minimum time interval within which there is little point in making forecasts. This is the period for which the stock of qualified manpower is already broadly determed" (Moser and Layard 1968). Again, "it seems reasonable to assume that manpower forecasts should be long term if they are to be useful for planning formal education" (Ahamad and Blaug 1973). Educational planners who have their doubts about the effectiveness and reliability of manpower forecasting point out that therein lies the basic dilemma in manpower planning. To be useful plans must be long term, but over 15- or 20-year periods the problems of predicting technological change or errors in the specification of model variables become much more severe. Ahamad and Blaug (1973) sum up this dilemma:

> We have the paradoxical situation that manpower forecasting should be long term to be really useful for educational decisions but, unfortunately, highly accurate forecasting is only possible in the short term or medium term.

We shall see below that the experiences and practices of individual countries well-versed in the use of manpower forecasts make them mindful of these problems; some allowances can be made by adapting plans to meet changing circumstances and by conducting short-term reviews. Thus, regular feedback, aided by built-in flexibility, can to some extent alleviate the difficulties of the time-scale of planning. In spite of such manipulations and revisions, some commentators still feel that basic rigidities in planning methods, when looking so far into the future, create insuperable difficulties. Ahamad and Blaug (1973) in a review of different countries' experiences with manpower forecasting found that "forecasting errors tend to be greater the longer the time horizon of the forecast". They quote Leser (1969):

> It would be a bold economist who would claim to foresee economic conditions and the tempo of economic change more than a decade ahead in view of rapid technical and institutional changes.

Ahamad and Blaug regard manpower forecasters as such "bold economists", in that "mindful of the long gestation lags in providing additional educational facilities, they have not hesitated to forecast 10 and even 20 years ahead" (Ahamad and Blaug 1973). They concede, however, that long-term forecasts might provide useful information to aid the decision making of individuals, and that in the absence of such an exploration of the future, students who choose courses on the basis of the current labour market positions of graduates could find the situation substantially altered by the time they join the labour force. This observation is obviously most pertinent for market economies.

The need for plans to be flexible and responsive to changing circumstances is one that is recognised both by manpower forecasters and by those more sceptical of their methods, such as Ahamad and Blaug, who advise:

> We feel that manpower forecasting should become much more of an ongoing activity and that short-term forecasts should be made fairly regularly at short-term intervals. This would afford greater flexibility and would also give more scope for improvement of the models used. In time we may even learn to predict accurately further into the future.

In common with all member countries of the CMEA the German Democratic Republic operates planning procedures over three interwoven time periods. The idea behind the CMEA arrangement is the synchronisation of planning activities to facilitate joint planning and the co-ordination of forecasting. The three time spans involved are:

- the long-term plan (15 years);
- the five-year plan;
- the national economic plan (annual).

The duration of the planning period is determined by the time span of the activity concerned, so that either the preceding educational stages or higher education can be adapted to meet changing circumstances. Sachse (1977) outlines the main differences in the three types of planning, particularly in relation to the accuracy and flexibility of each:

Long-term planning of the development of university and college-trained personnel is of a conceptual character and forms the precondition for basic changes in higher education. Planning is subject to a process of continual improvement and is, within certain limits, still flexible. The five-year plan contains a more precise definition of requirements and of the educational measures; this is then converted in the annual plan into the organised placement of trained graduates and fixing of the annual level of admissions.

The five-year plan and the annual plan in the GDR have legal force in respect to their implementation. The assessment of the demand for qualified manpower takes place in the framework of the five-year economic plan. Summary information on planning computations for this period was given in table 6.8.

In the first planning document prepared for Poland, various indicators were included that referred to the system of higher education. This was the first three-year Economic Reconstruction Plan, prepared in 1946 for the period 1947-49. Since that time the planning authorities in Poland have prepared five medium-term development plans and three versions of the long-range plan for periods covering 15-20 years. Plans in Poland now cover the years up to 2000, the latest being the "Poland 2000" report prepared by the Research and Forecasting Committee of the Polish Academy of Sciences.

A real base for "anticipatory" planning of education with regard to the future needs of the economy for qualified personnel was provided by the first long-range plan that covered the period 1961-75, prepared at the end of the 1950s. The employment and education planning system initiated in the late 1960s allowed for a feedback effect between economic sectors and education, "thus acquiring the characteristics of effective planning" (Kluczynski and Jozefowicz 1977). Three versions of the long-term demand for highly qualified personnel were prepared for 1960-80, 1965-85 and 1975-90 by the Inter-Ministry Committee using this kind of feedback. The increased demand for university-trained personnel suggested in consecutive forecasts was similar to the trend towards "raising the ceiling of the desirable level of employment of university-trained personnel" (Kluczynski and Jozefowicz 1977). Table 6.9 shows the results of consecutive forecasts of the demand for university-educated personnel.

In Polish planning practices, qualified manpower balance sheets are prepared for annual, five-year and longer periods. The annual qualified manpower balance sheets are produced by the Planning Commission of the Council of Ministers in the course of preparing the national economic plan. Five-year qualified manpower balance sheets are usually prepared twice: first, at the draft stage of the five-year economic plan and second, after the plan is approved. In the second exercise, the balances are drawn up in order:

"(1) to estimate the demand for qualified personnel on the basis of the objectives and tasks set in the five-year plan;

(2) to confront this demand with the potentialities of the regions, especially with respect to the supply of school graduates; and

(3) to determine the general trends in the policy of employment of school graduates"(Kluczynski and Jozefowicz 1977).

Table 6.9: Required employment in the public sector of personnel with university education according to different forecasts listed in chronological order of their preparation (Poland)

(thousands of persons)

	1970	1975	1980	1985
Long-range plan for 1960-1980	550	696	860	-
Planning Commission	491	716	817	910
Long-range plan for 1971-1985	558	742	944	1 134
Inter-Ministry Committee	502[a]	791	1 031	1 321

Source: Kluczynski and Jozefovich (1977), table 15.

[a] actual position.

In Poland, the annual and five-year balance sheets are regarded as important instruments of current employment policy, but it is recognised that they cannot provide a basis for changing the number and occupational structure of qualified specialists. This function is performed by long-range qualified personnel balance sheets that are prepared for periods of at least a decade, which is regarded as the minimum feasible lead time.

In Hungary early manpower plans (around 1950) were formulated on a short-term basis. There were two main reasons for a short-time horizon. First, in the 15-20 years following the end of the Second World War the manpower situation in Hungary was characterised by a severe shortage of highly qualified personnel. Because of the large number of vacancies in all occupational areas at this time, there was felt to be little need for a longer-term assessment of demand. Secondly, at this time no long-term plan for the economy had been developed. Thus, there was no forecast of economic and social development on which manpower plans could be based (Iván 1977). From 1965 onwards, manpower plans covered more distant time horizons - as far, in fact, as 1980. As in the German Democratic Republic and especially in Poland, annual and medium-term plans of manpower requirements are regarded as being most useful for manpower management, but are not seen as relevant or effective, compared with longer-term plans, for use in educational planning. Educational calculations are now made in Hungary not only for the period of the long-term plan (1970-1990) but also up to the year 2000.

For the Netherlands the RABAK and WORSA studies have already been referred to in Chapter 5. The RABAK (1975) forecast consisted of two parts: one part in which the over-all demand for university graduates was forecast, and one in which demand is forecast by discipline. This study covered the period up to 1990 and forecast the supply of graduates as well as the demand. Table 6.10 shows the forecast demand for and supply of university graduates in the Netherlands by discipline.

Table 6.10: University graduates forecasts of demand and supply (thousands) (Netherlands)

	1980 supply	1980 demand	1990 supply	1990 demand
Theology	5.6	4.3	7.4	4.3
Arts and literature including psychology and education	20.0	17.3	39.0	22.4
Medicine	23.7	23.4	31.3	29.8
Dentistry	4.7	5.6	7.5	6.3
Veterinary science	2.4	1.8	3.2	2.0
Science	20.0	17.0	40.2	22.5
Technical science	31.5	22.5	61.2	31.6
Agricultural science	5.1	4.1	11.0	6.5
Law	23.5	15.1	47.6	19.0
Economics	15.3	12.3	29.8	20.3
Social science	10.1	8.0	28.0	16.9
total	160.0	130.0	320.0	190.0

Source: Ritzen (1977), table VIII.4.

The WORSA (1975) study forecast that the number of new admissions to university would stabilise after 1978 at around 23,300. Forecasts of first year admissions for 1979 and 1990 and the total enrolment in those years are given in table 6.11. While RABAK estimates university enrolment in 1980 to be 170,000, the WORSA puts this number at around 130,000. For 1990, however, the forecasts of enrolment in the two studies differ by only 5,000 students. Both of these forecasts of supply and demand in the Netherlands adopted the time span of the 15-year forecast - 1975-1990.

Riese's (1967) study of the Federal Republic of Germany was based on data on student stocks and graduates up to 1964-65. (The background to this forecast is summarised in Chapter 5 of this book.) Riese estimated the demand for highly educated manpower and the supply of graduates up to 1981-82 in this study: his main findings are summarised in figure 6.2. The upper parallel lines show the overall estimates of the annual demand for new entrants to the graduate labour market (high and low forecasts of this demand are given). The lower horizontal line represents replacement demand. Figure 6.2 shows that for the FRG, in this study at least, a growing gap is forecast between the demand for and supply of highly qualified manpower.

Table 6.11: Forecasts of first year students and total enrolment 1979, 1990 (thousands) (Netherlands)

	First-year admissions		Enrolment	
	1979	1990	1979[1]	1990
Theology	.3	.3	1.9	1.8
Arts and literature	7.0	6.8	40.2	47.0
Medicine	1.8	1.8	12.8	12.9
Dentistry	.5	.5	2.7	2.7
Veterinary science	.2	.2	1.0	.9
Maths and physics	3.1	3.1	16.4	19.5
Technical sciences	3.1	3.0	16.5	18.1
Agriculture	1.0	1.0	5.1	6.4
Law	2.8	2.7	14.7	15.7
Economics	1.8	1.8	9.4	10.3
Social and political science	1.7	1.6	9.8	9.7
total	23.3	22.8	130.3	145.0

Source: Ritzen (1977), table VIII.1.

[1] Without restructuring of university education.

In Sweden forecasts do not at present look further ahead than the period 1975-80. Thus they could not be used for exact calculations of educational capacity to meet specific manpower requirements, even if the need for such calculations were felt (Bergendal 1977). The main reason for this rather short time horizon is the absence of suitable data. The Forecasting Institute is currently prearing a forecast of the supply of and demand for graduates in the 1980s, based on the census of 1970 and on the 1975 long-term plan.

Table 6.12 shows the numbers employed, or expected to be employed, in the major occupational groups in Sweden as a result of the calculations of the U68 Commission. The principles involved in calculating the new recruitment to be met from the education system were summarised earlier in this chapter and were illustrated in figure 6.1. Table 6.13 shows the results of these calculations and gives the estimated need for new recruitment from the Swedish educational system.

Figure 6.2

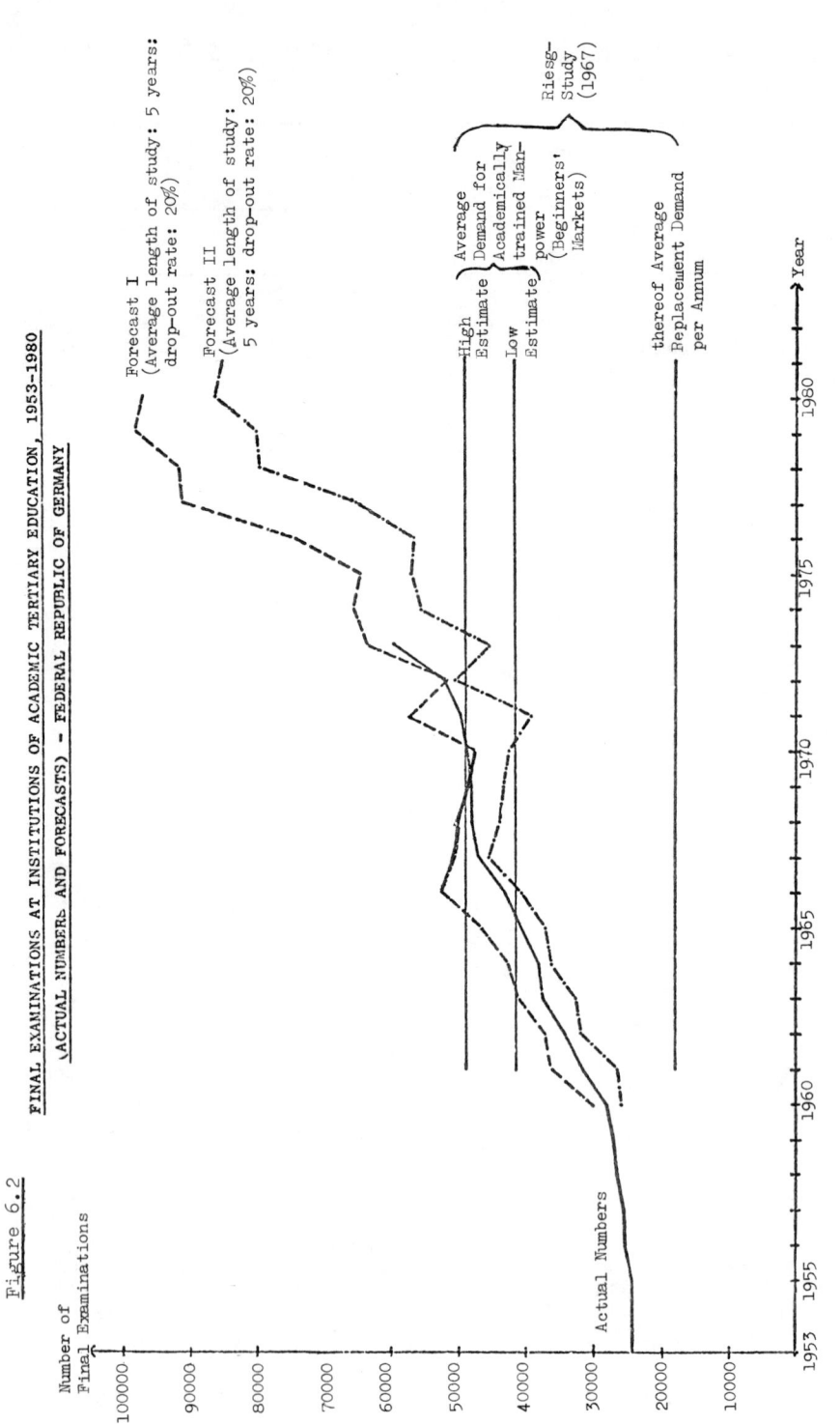

FINAL EXAMINATIONS AT INSTITUTIONS OF ACADEMIC TERTIARY EDUCATION, 1953-1980 (ACTUAL NUMBERS AND FORECASTS) - FEDERAL REPUBLIC OF GERMANY

Source: "Hufner et al (1977) Chapter 9.

Table 6.12

NUMBER OF GAINFULLY EMPLOYED IN MAJOR OCCUPATIONAL GROUPS 1960-80 (ROUND FIGURES) (SWEDEN)

Occupational group	1960	1970	1980
Technical work	168000	252000	331000
Medical care	108000	193000	285000
Educational work	81000	124000	166000
Other natural scientific, social scientific, humanistic and military work	80000	122000	173000
Administrative work	69000	88000	109000
Office work	275000	370000	423000
Commercial work	317000	326000	287000
Agriculture and forestry	505000	306000	166000
Communications	226000	217000	201000
Manufacturing	1165000	1147000	1032000
Services	316000	381000	422000
Total	3311000	3528000	3536000

Source: Bergendal (1977), Table 2.18

Table 6.13

THE NEED FOR NEW RECRUITMENT FROM THE EDUCATIONAL SYSTEM (SWEDEN)

Occupational group	1960/65	1965/70	1970/75	1975/80
Technical work	31000	43000	52000	53000
Medical care	33000	50000	59000	71000
Educational work	23000	32000	38000	40000
Other natural scientific, social scientific, humanistic and military work	16000	22000	27000	33000
Administrative work	2000	4000	6000	7000
Office work	87000	85000	86000	90000
Commercial work	44000	37000	33000	26000
Agriculture and forestry	25000	27000	17000	10000
Communications	27000	28000	27000	22000
Manufacturing	149000	11000	109000	112000
Services	47000	40000	43000	43000
Total	485000	479000	497000	506000

Source: Bergendal (1977), Table 2.20

In conclusion, educational planning, whether it involves manpower forecasting or the estimation of future student flows, must, to be effective, have at least one eye on the long-term future. Because of the time span of formal education, manpower developments and changes of trend have to be identified well in advance. Schools and universities take time to build, teachers need to be trained and the time-lag between a cohort entering one educational level and emerging as graduates all mean that the educational planner must both be aware of, and make quantified estimates of, the future course of events. The further one looks ahead the more uncertain it is that what is predicted will come to pass. "The future is uncertain and the point of making a forecast, whether of manpower or anything else, is to reduce the margin of uncertainty of future outcomes" (Ahamad and Blaug 1973). It is generally recognised that a certain amount of accuracy is lost by looking ahead 15 or 20 years, but if flexibility is built into long-range plans so that planning can react quickly to newly identified developments, there may still be plenty of room for the decision maker to manoeuvre.

Converting manpower forecasts into plans for the educational system can be a complicated business, but it is still only one step towards implementation. Perhaps the most important problem involved in implementing manpower-based plans for higher education in the real world is to orientate students in such a way that their own educational decisions are taken in the light of the best available information about the needs of the economy. Broadly speaking, the number of students entering the various branches of higher education can be regulated either by competitive examination for a limited number of places or by guidance and counselling to ensure that student wishes correspond at least approximately to social needs. The ways in which various countries deal with this problem are discussed in the next chapter.

CHAPTER 7

The implementation of manpower-based plans for higher education

Once it is decided how many places need to be provided in each of the main branches of higher education the final stage is to put these plans into effect, or more precisely to make adequate arrangements for the plans to be administered. As with the other aspects of manpower planning, the ways in which this can be done depend very much on the socio-political, legal and administrative arrangements in individual countries. In some cases it will be possible to determine by legislative or administrative fiat the number of students in each subject area on a year-to-year basis. More frequently, less direct methods of control will be necessary. For example it may be possible to provide financial incentives through the use of scholarships, special student subsidies, subsidies to higher education institutions and so on. In other cases the planning authorities have only the instruments of counselling and information dissemination.

The most widespread method of implementing manpower plans and of relating the social demand for places in higher education to employment opportunities is through the medium of vocational guidance and student counselling. In terms of the theoretical framework given in Chapters 3 and 4 one function of counselling is to try and ensure that educational provision based on the social demand for places will roughly correspond to society's needs for qualified manpower. These needs can of course be indicated either by manpower forecasting activities or by the trend of employment opportunities on the labour market. It might even be argued that full vocational guidance, based on accurate assessment of needs, would remove any contradiction between educational plans based on social demand and those based on manpower forecasts: there are, after all, few students in higher education who wish to be unemployed or misemployed after graduation.

This chapter discusses the arrangements which various countries make to facilitate vocational guidance and counselling and to implement policy-oriented manpower plans. It also examines the contention that the provision of information to students will by itself help to solve the problems of adjusting social demand to meet manpower requirements. Our starting point, however, is an examination of the difficulties caused by time-lags and rigidities in the operations of the labour market. Since market economies by their very nature rely to a great extent on market forces, which are believed to influence students, graduates, employed personnel and employers by means of remuneration and employment opportunities, provided information is available, these factors are of obvious importance.

The market mechanism - the economist's usual shorthand to depict the interdependency of the supply and demand for any good or service is to focus on the relationship between demand as a negative function of price on the one hand, and supply as a positive function of price on the other. When applied to the labour market, _ceteris paribus_, these operations can be represented as:

Demand for qualified manpower (D) = negative f (price of qualified manpower)

Supply of qualified manpower (S) = positive f (price of qualified manpower)

The graphic representation of the labour market for qualified manpower in an equilibrium position is given by figure 7.1. The point at which demand (DD) and supply (SS) curves intersect gives the equilibrium price of qualified manpower. In this highly simplified example, the equilibrium price of highly qualified manpower is given as OX. At this price the number of highly qualified personnel prepared to offer their services on the labour market is equal to the number that employers are prepared to hire at this price (or salary level). This number is given by OY.

Figure 7.1

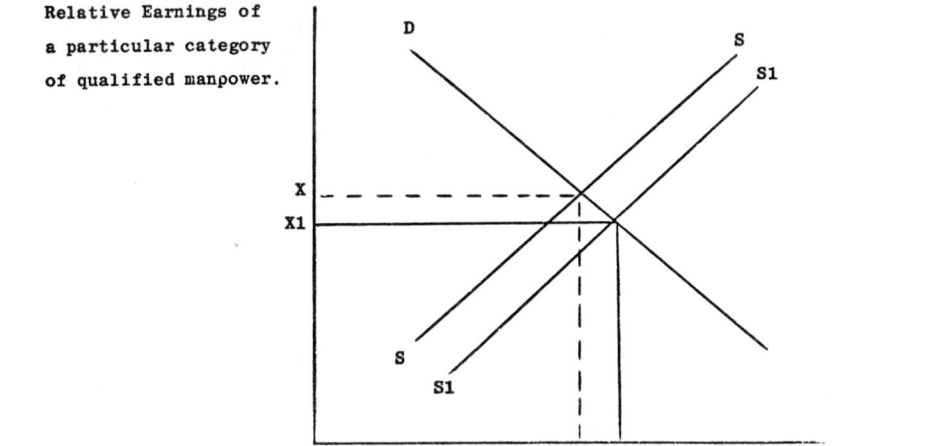

SUPPLY AND DEMAND FOR QUALIFIED MANPOWER IN EQUILIBRIUM

If the equilibrium position shown in figure 7.1 is disturbed for some reason, the speed with which adjustments take place to reach a new equilibrium is of obvious importance for the efficient allocation of resources. The equilibrium could be disturbed, for example, because of an increased demand by employers for highly qualified manpower due to economic growth, or because of a greater supply of personnel from universities. If for instance, we assume an increase in supply because of expansion of higher education, the supply curve would shift to S1 - S1 and the new equilibrium would be reached at a wage rate of OX1. If new graduates were reluctant to accept this fall in their relative earnings it would result in the number Y - Y1 being unemployed or at best under- or misemployed. The time-lag involved in the realignment of supply and demand needs to be as short as possible if market adjustments are going, by themselves, to be able to produce a satisfactory new equilibrium.

The concept of the "cobweb cycle" illustrates one possible type of adjustment that has obvious economic and social disadvantages. Essentially the "cobweb" is a graphical representation of the effects of time-lags on readjustments in supply and demand in the movement towards a new equilibrium. Figure 7.2 shows that a new equilibrium position is eventually reached by a series of price fluctuations, each one of which causes employers or qualified personnel (or would-be students, depending on the time-lag involved) to over-react.

Figure 7.2

COBWEB CYCLE ADJUSTMENTS IN SUPPLY AND DEMAND

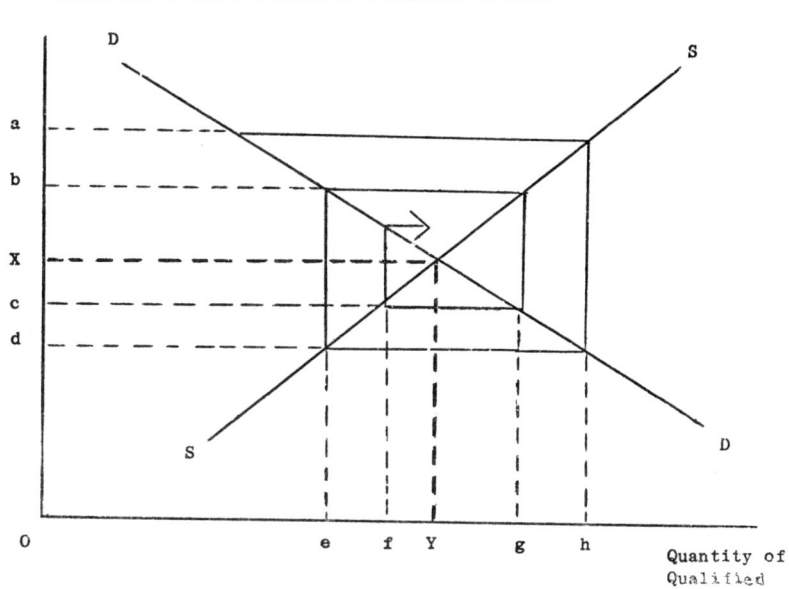

This model shows that under some assumptions about the operations of the labour market, it will be a long time before a new equilibrium is reached. In the intervening period there will be alternating shortages and surpluses of qualified manpower on the labour market. Empirical evidence from the United States of this type of adjustment for some categories of qualified manpower is given by Freeman (1971).

"Cobweb" type adjustments in the market for highly qualified manpower occur when the time-lag between a decision to expand the supply of manpower and the time when new graduates are ready for employment is so long that changes in earnings may cause students or employers to over-react, so that shortages are turned into surpluses and earnings fluctuate wildly. Thus, for example, a shortage of accountants on the labour market, which is revealed by high earnings, rapid promotion, etc., may influence many students to enrol in accountancy courses, perhaps more than enough to compensate for the shortage. A situation of over-supply will then result. The situation is obviously made worse if students and potential students are responding to information that is some years out of date.

The question that has to be faced by any government that aims to regulate higher education in accordance with economic needs is whether it is more efficient to attempt to restore equilibrium through the use of manpower planning techniques or by other means. The point of disagreement between planners in favour of manpower forecasting and those against it is not whether the time-lags described above exist or not (clearly they do and are important: students, employers and educational planners generally base their own decisions on out-of-date information). Nor is there any disagreement about the need to remedy shortages or surpluses of manpower as quickly as possible so as to make the most efficient use of resources. The fundamental disagreement is about whether manpower forecasting and its implementation is an appropriate mechanism to remedy imbalances and to eliminate the uncertainty of time-lags. Those who favour manpower forecasting argue that the market is unable to remedy shortages and surpluses on its own, and a thorough assessment of the country's manpower requirements in the future, backed up by translation into places in higher education is the only way to allocate scarce resources efficiently.

The view of economists who favour the free market is that there is not a rigid relationship between education and occupation, and the short-term adjustments are possible if the price mechanism encourages employers to substitute a category of labour in plentiful supply for one that is in short supply. Thus the effective time-lag between a disequilibrium appearing and the supply of labour reacting to it can be reduced, and the market turns out to be able to adjust itself without any severe disturbance.

Both views, however, rely to a large extent on good information, that is on informing would-be students of career opportunities; even if the "perfect" knowledge assumed in theoretical market economies is unattainable, some notion of likely outcomes must be present. We now turn, therefore, to examine the arrangements made for vocational guidance and counselling and graduate placement facilities in centrally planned and market economies. In the former, as we shall see, an attempt is made to orientate would-be students towards expected future manpower needs.

In the latter, whilst information concerning likely employment prospects is in many cases an important component of counselling and guidance, the information itself is less precise. Greater weight is placed on encouraging informed decision making by students themselves, in the light of their own academic interests and the current labour market demand for various types of skills.

Guidance, counselling and job placement in the German Democratic Republic

In the German Democratic Republic the planned admission of students to university and the planned placement of graduates in employment is accomplished through a system of information, advice and guidance with a view to the harmonisation of students' vocational preferences on the one hand and the requirements of society on the other.

It is believed that detailed information on the needs of society, the encouragement of interest in needed disciplines and employment areas and the "steering" of young people towards them are all necessary to co-ordinate individual preferences and societal needs. "Any uncontrolled development leads to human disappointments and waste of societal resources if it is known from the start that no realistic possibilities of employment will be available" (Sachse 1977).

The underlying theme of all vocational guidance in the German Democratic Republic is thus to attempt to bring the vocational aspirations of young people into line with the needs of society. Employment opportunities and opportunities in higher education derived from the prepared manpower plans are made known to young people, and they are encouraged to act in accordance with these social needs. The preparation and recruiting of applicants for higher education are part of the organised vocational guidance system. Figure 7.3 shows for both higher education aspirants and for graduates how individual preferences and manpower plans are reconciled.

The orientation, preparation and guidance of young people prior to admission to higher education institutions can be considered in five stages:

(1) Intensive vocational information and orientation begins at the start of the eleventh grade of the extended secondary school (the matriculation examination is taken after the twelfth grade - see figure 7.3). The following material is available to students for information at this stage:

(a) university and college guidebooks which describe occupations by content and employment opportunities;

(b) the planned targets for admission of students to individual subject disciplines;

(c) an "orientation table" on the ratio of places in higher education to applicants in previous years. The idea is for students to draw their own conclusions on trends of shortages and surpluses of applicants for different disciplines.

Figure 7.3

TIMETABLE OF STUDY CONTROL AND PLACEMENT OF GRADUATES IN THE GERMAN DEMOCRATIC REPUBLIC

Study orientation	Extended upper secondary school (EOS)			Admission to study	Universities and colleges			
	11th grade application	12th grade admission	Final applications		First year	Penultimate study year	Beginning of the final year	Systematic placement of graduates
	Ascertainment of preferences	Guiding of preferences			Occupational orientation	Start of steering and placement discussions	Conclusion of employment contracts	
	Central evaluation							

Planning of new admissions and influence on choice of studies according to demand indicated by the Ministry of Higher Education

Preparation for the engagement of graduates by future employers

Planning of the expected graduates by the Ministry of Higher Education

Balancing of jobs and graduates with the co-operation of the Ministry of Higher Education and central authorities

Central control of the planned preparation and placement of graduates

Planning by the State Planning Commission of the demand for university and college-level manpower and admissions and/or growth of the number of students

Source: Sachse 1977.

On the basis of this information, vocational guidance sessions are organised. In each province an institution of higher education has been established to carry out vocational guidance for all disciplines through the use of experts in each subject area.

(2) At the next stage, students register their preferences for studying a certain discipline (a second choice may be indicated). General personal information is also submitted at this stage. As a result of these registrations, the first balance of students' choices and available places in higher education is drawn up by computer.

The long-term preparation for the admission of young people to higher education means that most would-be students are aware of the country's manpower requirements and the prospects of admission to higher education. "The result is that individual preferences are, to a large extent, brought into harmony with the requirements of society" (Sachse 1977).

There are, however, a number of matching problems: there are disciplines, for example, for which more young people regularly apply than there are places available and vice versa. In recent years those disciplines with more applicants than places include biology, psychology, pharmacy, construction, transport, architecture, medicine, veterinary medicine, law and journalism. Too few applicants have in recent years applied for mathematics, physics, polytechnical teaching and similar disciplines. The similarity to the proclaimed shortage of students in mathematically-based science subjects in some Western European countries is striking.

(3) At the third stage efforts are made to resolve such problems of over- and under-subscription to different disciplines. Fresh vocational guidance discussions take place with students and their parents, to try to shift applicants from overcrowded subject areas to those that are under-subscribed. Experience in the German Democratic Republic has shown that such renewed counselling usually leads to closer harmony between student choice and manpower needs.

(4) Students now submit actual applications for higher education by forwarding the required personal documents. To some extent the applications procedure is interwoven with actual admission. Schools are able to recommend strongly those applicants who receive the citation "particularly suited for studies". This procedure guarantees study places to the most able applicants and eases the pressure on selection by universities and colleges. Approximately 30 per cent of all applicants are recommended in this way.

(5) The fifth stage is the actual admission of applicants to universities and colleges. The numbers admitted are determined by each institution's plan of enrolments. For a high proportion of applicants, admission is determined immediately - those highly recommended by their schools and others with good matriculation marks. For a few disciplines separate admission examinations are arranged. All applicants not admitted to university or college are involved in discussions designed to orient them to vacant places on other courses and to determine their future careers.

In the planning of admissions, universities and colleges are given guidance on the number of graduates they should produce in each discipline. An appropriately larger number of applicants are admitted to the first year of study to make allowance for student wastage.

We have seen earlier how admission to university or college in the German Democratic Republic is closely related to employment opportunities for graduates. Each entrant to higher education has the guarantee that, subject to satisfactory performance in his studies, he will be offered a job upon graduation corresponding very closely to his qualifications. The first step in placing graduates in jobs consists of estimating the numbers expected to qualify in each discipline. They can then be "steered" to the specific employment areas defined as having the most urgent need for their services. "The steering of graduates ... is materially and ideologicially stimulated on the basis of the most effective method. Appropriate salary adjustments, recently also more and more measures for the provision of housing, child-care facilities and other benefits in working and living conditions, support planning so that in the end the targets can be attained" (Sachse 1977).

The first stage in the process takes place two-and-a-half years prior to graduation of the age-cohort concerned, and involves the elaboration by the Ministry of Higher Education of a preliminary balance in which the probable number of graduates available, by discipline and institution, is compared with the corresponding demands of manpower users. At this stage it is possible to identify subject areas where supply and demand are matched as well as emerging problems of which notice has to be taken. Thus "the problems and possible imbalances are sorted out and the programme for the placement of graduates is gradually worked out"(Sachse 1977).

Eighteen months before students sit the state final examination, placement discussions commence. This enables the future graduate to conclude his employment contract a year before graduation and gives employing agencies advance information on the fulfilment of their own manpower plans. An important step towards the actual placement of graduates in employment is the preparation by employers of "conditions of placement". This document constitutes the offer made by the employer and contains information concerning the place of work, duties, remuneration, promotion possibilities and any social benefits. These placement conditions form the basis for recruitment. Suitable graduates are selected on the basis of personal discussions between university and college teachers and representatives of employing agencies, and employment contracts are concluded.

There has in the past been no difficulty in finding suitable employment for graduates. In 1971, for example, just over 50 per cent of vacancies for university graduates were in fact filled by university graduates. The remainder of vacancies were filled by college graduates, technicians, etc. (Sachse 1977). Thus, in these circumstances some vacancies for graduates have to be filled with personnel with lower educational qualifications. From 1970 to 1975 the number of graduates in the economy rose by some 50 per cent. Some graduates are now being engaged for types of jobs which, owing to earlier shortages, were previously filled by personnel with lower qualifications. This change has caused difficulties in adjusting students' expectations and aspirations to match the new situation. These expectations have naturally been strongly influenced by the graduate employment opportunities of previous years: the filling of graduate level posts by non-graduates has led to some students regarding these positions as of inferior (non-graduate) status. This problem is one also experienced in the market economies of Western Europe.

Guidance, counselling and job placement in Poland

In Poland, as in the German Democratic Republic, "the basic need for a rational link between manpower policy and educational policy arose from the strategy of full employment" (Kluczynski and Jozefowicz 1977). The economic strategy of the centrally planned economies of Eastern Europe has as a basic doctrine a management of human resources to ensure full employment. It is not surprising then, to find that considerable emphasis is put on the placement of graduates in suitable occupations as an integral part of manpower planning policy.

In the past in Poland there have been considerable discrepancies between education plans based on manpower forecasts and the implementation of these plans. The discrepancies can largely be accounted for by the repeated reforms of the educational system. These reforms were in a sense forced upon the authorities by the current needs of the economy and the demand for qualified manpower, or by the inability of the economy to always ensure the full and rational employment of young people.

One characteristic of the Polish situation which appears to contrast with the situation in the German Democratic Republic, is the relatively high proportion of graduates who do not take up employment in the field of their specialism. The long cycle of education, combined sometimes with the lack of early vocational guidance and orientation, as well as occasional errors in planning the targets for the education system have resulted in between 10 and 30 per cent of graduates not taking up employment in the occupation for which they have been trained. It should be noted that in Western Europe a figure of over 70 per cent of graduates taking up jobs closely related to their academic specialism would be considered remarkably high.

Although the attention which was given in the past to vocational guidance and orientation at the pre-university level is now regarded as inadequate (Kluczynski and Jozfowicz 1977), considerable attention has been devoted for some time to the placement of university graduates in appropriate employment. The system of job placement was first introduced in Poland in 1950, with little reference to economic plans. Job placement at this time was performed mainly by administrative instruments of employment direction and allocation, assessed on the basis of an inflexible and often inaccurate perception of manpower requirements. This system was abolished in 1956 in favour of an employment-service operated job guidance and clearance system, which was kept in operation until 1963. The present system of the planned employment of graduates was adopted in a Parliament Act of February 1964, and operates within the following terms of reference:

- to determine which graduates should become eligible for employment placement, after first identifying the most important skills needed for set targets in Poland;

- graduates who obtain employment through this placement scheme must stay in their jobs for at least three years;

- graduates will be directed to their first employment by specially appointed representatives of the Labour Ministry who are assigned to individual institutions of higher education.

In the decade 1964 to 1974, just under 300,000 full-time students graduated from universities in Poland. Of these 220,000 graduated in the faculties covered by the Act of 1964. Ninety per cent of this group were directed to jobs through the system of planned employment.

While the core components of the current pre-planned graduate employment system bear some similarity to the systems in operation in the 1950s and early 1960s (i.e. allocation on the basis of anticipated manpower demand, the identification of crucial areas of job placement, and the obligation on the graduate to stay for three years in the job to which he has been directed) the Act of 1964, together with its subsequent amendments introduced more flexible and liberal procedures for graduate placement.

Three categories of prearranged job placement operate under the conditions of the 1964 Act. These are:

(a) the industrial grant programme;

(b) starting agreements;

(c) employment direction.

The first category of prearranged placement is designed to attract, by means of economic incentives, the best specialists eligible to meet the vacancies of employing agencies. The grants available under the industrial grant programme are on average 20-30 per cent higher than the stipends offered by the academic authorities. The regulations provide for certain sanctions to be applied in the event of the agreement being broken by either student or employer. Between 30 and 60 per cent of graduates were placed in their first job under this form of sponsorship agreement in individual years of the last decade.

The "starting agreement" procedure attracts the smallest proportion of graduates. These agreements are usually negotiated towards the end of a student's course of study by students who wish to obtain security against the risk of imbalances between employment opportunities and the number of qualified applicants for a given occupation. Under this procedure too, the employing agency gives financial aid to the student.

Graduates who have not received industrial grants or opted for "starting agreements" receive "employment directions" from the representative of the Ministry of Labour assigned to individual higher education institutions. These graduates are free to make their own choice of occupation from among those vacancies registered with his institution.

Kluczynski and Jozefowicz (1977) identify a number of shortcomings in the present system of job placement. However, they recognise that the system in Poland, while attempting to implement manpower-based plans, allows a considerable margin of autonomy for the behaviour of individuals, educational institutions and employers. It may well be this autonomy that accounts for the main shortcomings which they outline. One problem has already been mentioned - the high proportion of graduates who take up jobs for which they have not been trained, in spite of the job placement schemes. It has also proved difficult to attract and settle specialists in areas of new development, owing to the inadequacy of suitable incentives, particularly in housing amenities. In addition, it is estimated that a significant proportion of the working time of graduates who are correctly placed is inefficiently used in performing tasks that could be delegated to less qualified staff. A further problem, not related to job placement, but which has to be taken notice of in implementing manpower plans, is the high level of student wastage in Polish higher education. It is estimated that drop-out from intra-mural studies exceeds 20 per cent of intake, while that from extra-mural studies exceeds 40 per cent.

Guidance, couselling and job placement in Romania

In Romania also it is claimed that "one of the important elements by which the training of highly qualified personnel is regulated is public opinion generally and the counselling and orientation services provided to candidates to higher education". (Pestisanu, et al 1977). Great efforts are made through the counselling services to ensure that individuals' wishes coincide with the social and economic needs of the nation. However, admission to full-time higher education is determined mainly on the basis of competitive entry examinations, and the number of places available in each subject area is determined according to estimated future manpower needs. Candidates who are unsuccessful in the examination for the faculty of their choice can opt to enter another faculty with less intensive competition for entry, or they can try again the following year.

Once admitted to universities and other colleges, students are provided with information about the career opportunities open to them. Each year a government commission seeks from all the main employing agencies details of the numbers of employees in each category of qualified manpower that they propose to recruit that year, and the geographical location of these vacancies. This information is provided to students who normally arrange the job they will enter during their final year of studies. Jobs are allocated on the basis of subject of specialisation and proved academic ability. In order to ensure a continuing concordance between the output of higher education and the needs of the economy increasing attention is being paid to the possibilities provided by permanent education.

Guidance, counselling and job placement in Hungary

The system of mass vocational guidance in Hungary is associated mainly with the first point of vocational decision (at 13-14 years of age) when a choice has to be made between three types of school - a choice that determines by and large the place the student will take in the social division of labour. Vocational aptitude tests are playing an increasingly important role in counselling and guidance in Hungary, especially in relation to admission to higher education. The state vocational guidance service functions under the direct control of Budapest council and the county councils and is equipped to conduct psychological tests.

The flexible nature of Hungarian policies in relation to manpower planning and education is summarised by Iván (1977). "The matching of education to the needs of the economy takes place through a free choice of career among the wide opportunities for employment. In such conditions, indirect influencing of the individual through an effectively functioning information and orientation system is of particular importance." While the size and composition of higher education in Hungary conforms to the forecast needs of the national economy, the plans are implemented largely through a system of open competitions for jobs. There are some doubts about the extent to which young graduates seeking jobs on their own succeed in finding employment in line with their education and training. A further difficulty is that the use of open competitions may not correspond to the needs of the economy. At the moment employers can invite applications without any restrictions.

Increasing emphasis therefore is now being placed on securing appropriate first employment for graduates. The prevailing belief is that young specialists starting on their careers need special assistance; in the interest of giving them a good start, the authorities must take care to assist them in the selection of their first job. "Their employment must not be left to an accidental meeting of demand and supply, though it may be supposed that in most cases advantageous solutions come about in this way and that many such opportunities are revealed which are inaccessible to central intervention" (Iván 1977).

Some students in Hungarian higher education are sponsored on their studies by an employer. The "enterprise-offered student grant" is a contractual relationship between the undergraduate and his future employer during the period of the student's studies. In return for a grant somewhat larger than that of the state scholarship, the student commits himself for a few years upon graduation to work for the enterprise offering the grants. The purpose of this system of grants is to channel specialists to certain jobs with major enterprises or to geographical regions poorly supplied with specialists.

The fact that higher education is designed to meet the economy's demand for specialised manpower sets limits on the number of students that can be admitted to each subject area. Because of an excess number of applications, young people have to be turned away from studying some disciplines, whereas in other subject areas less talented students are admitted. It is also a matter of concern that in subjects with a very limited capacity the number of applicants often considerably exceeds the prescribed number of admissions. Even candidates who achieve a near-maximum number of points in the entrance examination may be unable to gain a place for the university subject of their choice in a given year. It can be seen, then, that the implementation of manpower plans in Hungary has a strong impact on the number of new entrants to higher education, but upon graduation employment opportunities are in general plentiful. The direction of graduates to jobs does not take place in any systematic way. Thus in Hungary the planning of output and the placement of graduates is left much more to individual choice than is the case in the German Democratic Republic or Poland.

Guidance, counselling and job placement in the Netherlands

General vocational counselling in the Netherlands is offered by 37 bureaux with 655 full-time workers (1974), mainly to students in primary and secondary education. In 1973, fewer than 15 per cent of all consultations were given to young people over the age of 18. Fewer than 1 per cent (900 consultations) were given to graduates or university students and only 2.5 per cent to those in senior technical training or higher vocational education. In the Netherlands vocational counselling does not constitute an important part of the higher education system - only students with difficulties consult vocational counsellors on their own initiative or are referred to them. If a graduate does receive guidance, it is generally as a result of a referral by the job placement service and is usually in connection with the fact that he or she has been unable to find employment.

While graduate unemployment in the 1950s and 1960s was of negligible proportions, the employment services had little knowledge of the "graduate sector" of the labour market; and so could offer little help to those few graduates who found themselves unemployed. In 1955 a "central point for academics" was established with the objective of assisting the employment service in its dealings with university graduates. In 1972 the "central point" was replaced by the BAA (Bureau Arbeidsvoorziening Academici) - a placement service for university graduates. Under the aegis of the BAA, 26 offices provide a job bank for graduates.

The BAA was established to make the labour market for university graduates and higher executive personnel less complex. It was felt that existing allocative instruments were inadequate to deal with a graduate labour market which was growing rapidly in size, and was becoming even more complex owing to the growing differentiation of occupations and subject disciplines. A major goal of the BAA is to reduce the number of unemployed university graduates and to limit the duration of unemployment, while attempting to facilitate a better match between supply and demand (Ritzen 1977).

In addition to its network of bureaux at universities and regional employment offices, the BAA offers a regular listing of vacancies, a periodical listing of university graduates in search of jobs and a registration and selection system. These services are aimed particularly at graduates interested in information on the labour market, many of whom do not require any assistance in the selection of information or in the application process, even though such assistance is available. The BAA does not intervene in applications; it is primarily concerned with providing information to allow the supply of graduates and the demand for their services to inter-react more efficiently.

The clientele of the BAA job banks appears to consist primarily of unemployed graduates seeking work and the underemployed seeking employment commensurate with their qualifications.

Apart from the BAA, no other specific measures exist that are geared exclusively to higher education graduates. However, there are other instruments in existence that are designed to promote the efficient allocation of manpower, and these also affect the position of graduates on the labour market to varying extents. Three subsidy instruments are in operation:

(a) wage supplements;

(b) 30 per cent wage-cost reimbursement;

(c) temporary jobs (TAP).

While all three can apply to highly qualified manpower, the temporary job regulations (TAP) are more relevant to higher education graduates than the other two instruments. The "30 per cent wage-cost reimbursement" applies mostly to graduates of senior vocational training and higher vocational education.

In 1973 and 1974 almost 1,200 higher education graduates were employed under the TAP regulations: the temporary jobs mechanism is estimated to employ between 20-25 per cent of all unemployed university graduates. The regulations provide for the full reimbursement of all salary costs for a maximim of six months with a maximum of $700 a month, but only in full-time or temporary government or semi-government jobs. The TAP is considered a useful instrument towards helping graduates to obtain permanent employment.

The wage supplement regulation is intended for those unemployed or those about to be unemployed who are willing to accept a full-time job below the wage rate of their previous job. Because of the restrictive conditions that apply to the wage supplement regulations few unemployed are eligible.

The 30 per cent wage-cost reimbursement regulation does not impose such severe restrictions. Under this arrangement the Government subsidises non-government employers for a period of six months to the extent of 30 per cent of wages up to a given maximum. This applies to a full-time permanent job given to an individual for whom placement is otherwise difficult. About 50 higher education graduates took advantage of this regulation in 1973 and 1974.

In general, therefore, vocational guidance is considered appropriate to only a very limited extent for university graduates and is entirely reactive to the current situation on the labour market. In this it contrasts markedly with the countries described so far in which efforts are made to orientate student numbers in accordance with estimated future needs of employers. With the exception of the placement service for university graduates (BAA) and the temporary jobs regulation such orientation services as do exist reach very few higher education students or graduates. Ritzen (1977) suggests that more could be done for university graduates in particular by way of providing information and advice on the labour market through in-service training, counselling and guidance. He also recommends the extension of the BAA scheme to cover higher vocational education graduates as well as its present clientele of university graduates.

Guidance, counselling and job placement
in the Federal Republic of Germany

In 1968 the Institut für Arbeitsmarkt - und Berufsforschung (IAB - Institute for Labour Market and Employment Research) was founded as part of the Bundesanstalt für Arbeit (Federal Employment Agency). Since then the institute has played a prominent role in providing up-to-date assessments of the short-run situation and long-term trends on various labour markets. The institute's function is restricted to what could be called an active monitoring of labour market conditions. Concrete measures of intervention are left to the respective departments of the federal and Länder governments or to the Federal Employment Agency itself, all of which are expected to react to the trends revealed by the Institute's work.

The Federal Employment Agency's responsibilities - beyond those of administering old-age and unemployment insurance schemes and placement services for the unemployed - extend to active measures such as devising and administering training and retraining schemes, and counselling and placement activities for prospective new entrants to the labour force. These activities take the form of individual counselling in the agency's regional offices, lectures to school-leavers and the publication of labour market trend assessments for pupils and students. "In general analytical terms, the efforts of the Federal Employment Agency are predominantly aimed at directly or indirectly influencing the actual and the prospective supply of labour according to presently manifested or anticipated demands emanating from public and private employers" (Hüfner, et al 1977).

In addition to the activities of the Federal Employment Agency, the supply of highly qualified manpower is also directly influenced through the medium of numerus clausus regulations in higher education institutions. The substantial increase in the number of young people entitled to enter higher education meant that capacity problems became increasingly severe in certain disciplines and institutions in the 1960s. Since between 80 and 90 per cent of young people meeting the formal entry requirements of academic tertiary education actually wanted to undertake it, admission restrictions had to be imposed on an ever-increasing number of fields of study in the late 1960s. By 1970-71 nearly all the faculties of medicine, pharmacy, psychology and architecture had met their capacity limits and therefore began to impose restrictions.

A centralised system of admission procedures was established in the early 1970s for half a dozen fields of study, regulating entry on a republic-wide scale. In addition, individual universities or even individual subject departments had to impose entry regulations of their own to cope with their capacity problems. Thus the Federal Republic has to some extent abandoned the dictates of planning on the basis of social demand: the principle of freedom of choice of institutions and fields of study for all those possessing the formal academic entry qualifications has been restricted by the imposition of numerus clausus regulations. Although officially the numerus clausus is determined by considerations of cost rather than by formal estimates of future qualified manpower needs, decisions about expansion to meet social demand are almost certainly indirectly influenced in certain subjects by manpower considerations, and by anticipated employment opportunities for graduates.

Guidance, counselling and job placement
in Sweden

The relationship between higher education and the manpower needs of society was first studied in Sweden in the 1930s by the Wicksell-Jerneman Commission. Its brief was to investigate the growing difficulties experienced by university graduates in finding jobs in the "intellectual professions". In rejecting the notion of a limited intake to higher education tied to manpower forecasts, the Commission recommended better information for future students on labour market prospects, and educational and vocational guidance as methods of easing employment difficulties. This emphasis on social demand moderated by guidance services has remained the essential basis of higher education planning in Sweden since that time.

The National Labour Market Board has offered vocational guidance in upper-secondary schools since the early 1940s. In the early part of the period vocational counsellors visited these schools from time to time and gave students information about the relationship between subject disciplines and the labour market. In the 1950s careers teachers were introduced into the then experimental comprehensive schools, to help pupils make occupational choices. During this period university students were offered vocational guidance in the form of lectures by teachers and counsellors and through various social activities arranged by student organisations.

These rather ad hoc arrangements were systematised in 1964 as a by-product of the parliamentary reform of upper-secondary education. An integrated approach to counselling in the secondary school was then introduced. Counselling was provided that year on the basis of co-operation between the labour market authorities and the school. The school welfare officer was made responsible for the practical co-ordination of the system, and was given the task of assisting the careers adviser from the labour market authorities in providing vocational orientation and study guidance.

At the beginning of the enrolments explosion in Sweden in the 1960s, the first concerted efforts were made to create a system for counselling and guidance which would reach every student in primary, secondary and higher education, as well as to serve would-be adult students already in employment. By the mid-1970s the implementation of the new arrangements is complete as far as young people are concerned. It is anticipated that the next few years will witness the build-up of similar resources for information and outreach activities for adults in work or staying at home (Bergendal 1977).

When in the early 1970s higher education graduates began to experience employment difficulties, the National Labour Market Board took a series of measures in an attempt to improve the situation. Within the employment agencies themselves more resources were devoted to a service geared to the needs of new graduates from universities and colleges. This was aimed both at graduates who were experiencing difficulties in finding employment corresponding to their qualifications, and at those whose subject specialism had a tenuous connection with employment. Personnel with specialised knowledge of the graduate labour market were posted to employment agencies in university towns. Although their main tasks were planning and information, there was a conscious effort on the part of the employment agencies to broaden the job horizons of student and graduate applicants towards considering new fields of employment.

One form of aid of which graduates avail themselves if they are unable to find jobs on their own or through the employment agencies is through a system of "employment training". In the past decade employment training has played an increasingly important part in Swedish employment policy. The State takes care of the costs of this form of occupational training and provides grants for students on the scheme. The training, which may range from a duration of two months to two years has three main objectives:

(a) to facilitate adjustment of the unemployed to new jobs and to provide individuals who may become unemployed in the near future with new skills;

(b) to help groups who have difficulty finding employment, such as the handicapped;

(c) to meet the need of the economy for trained manpower, particularly where technological or structural changes necessitate the acquisition of new skills.

Employment training in Sweden has been found to be an effective means of solving specific unemployment problems. Currently more than 2 per cent of the labour force is taking such training every year. Among those taking part in employment training schemes are a high proportion of graduates: table 7.1 shows the numbers of graduates from universities and colleges who have undergone employment training since 1969.

Table 7.1: Number of graduates in employment training in Sweden

1969	1970	1971	1972	1973	1974
750	1 100	1 400	2 200	2 500	2 500

Where there are no regular job opportunities and when employment training is not possible, measures may be taken to create employment opportunities. In recent years the aim has been to develop relief work projects in order to meet the demands of new categories of unemployed. Under this scheme a considerable number of new graduates have been offered temporary jobs, particularly in the administrative and service sector of the economy. The intention of the scheme is to give meaningful employment to those taking part, taking into account their previous educational and work experience. The scheme also serves the purpose of practice and further training as a preparation for the transfer into normal employment.

It can be seen that like the Netherlands, Sweden attacks the problems of the transition from full-time education to the labour market in a number of ways. The most comprehensive is the system of vocational counselling and guidance that pervades all levels of education and is soon to be fully extended to adults. In addition, through employment training schemes and temporary employment opportunities serious attempts are made to harmonise policies for the supply of qualified manpower with the available employment opportunities. This is done through the availability of information, training and retraining of graduates and non-graduates alike. In Sweden, as in the Netherlands, the use of numerus clausus at the entry point to higher education can also effectively limit student numbers in subject areas where employment difficulties are being experienced by graduates.

The role of counselling

"It is the task of the counsellor in schools and universities to help the student to analyse his own situation, his aptitudes, interests and requirements, and to assess his situation in the light of the requirements and of the opportunities offered by different courses of education and different tasks in working life" (Bergendal 1977).

While this claim is applicable to all the counselling systems surveyed in this chapter, it is evident from the review of experience that some countries take counselling a step further. For instance, it is debatable whether a counsellor should have a directive or non-directive function. Policy makers in different countries have given different answers to this. Many argue that the counsellor's role is to propose to the individual student a set of alternatives according to his or her ability, choice of studies, interests and so on but not to give advice on which might be best for the student in the light either of his attributes or the needs of the economy. Others maintain that, in order to be effective, it is necessary not only to provide information in a neutral way, but actively to advise, guide and "orientate" the student with regard to possible alternatives. The debate becomes sharper when counselling attempts to harmonise individual aspirations and the manpower requirements of the economy.

Some planners have expressed the hope that accurate information to students and prospective students will prove to be an adequate method of achieving a reasonable balance between graduate output and the needs of the economy. According to this view, restricted admission to educational institutions could then be phased out since students would act in a rational way. However, it is evident that choices and preferences between various educational options are determined by a combination of rational and more or less irrational factors. In Hungary, grossly over-subscribed departments continue to attract highly qualified school-leavers who stand little chance of gaining admission, while other subject areas could accommodate them. In the German Democratic Republic, prospective students are aware of the relative difficulties in gaining a place in different departments but may still have to be re-orientated towards less popular areas at the second stage of the applications process. The same over-application occurs in the _numerus clausus_ faculties of the Federal Republic of Germany and the Netherlands. It may be claimed in the market economies concerned that more resources invested in information and guidance could mitigate the situation; but this does not appear altogether likely. There are convincing theoretical arguments to support a pessimistic view of the efficiency of information and guidance as a regulator of the over-all relationship between education and the economy. This is so, especially in the market economies that rely primarily on social demand as the basis for the provision of publicly subsidised higher education. Given the lack of over-all co-ordination, prospective students in the market economies who learn of a forecast shortage or over-supply in a particular occupation cannot, as individual decision makers, anticipate the simultaneous decisions of all the other prospective students who must make similar choices; nor can individual counsellors help them. The centrally planned economies are at least able to co-ordinate entry to higher education, but it is evident that this does not resolve all difficulties.

The graduates themselves are confronted by a variety of job placement and counselling schemes in the different countries surveyed. These schemes can be regarded as a continuum from, at one extreme, early job placement of students before graduation, coupled with guarantees of full employment; to, at the other extreme, optional counselling and advice facilities if students and graduates wish to avail themselves of the service. As has been repeated many times in this book, the actual system in operation will reflect the socio-political framework within which the higher education system operates. In spite of this basic constraint, there are few who would argue with Bergendal's (1977) observation on the objectives of counselling and guidance:

> The purpose of educational and vocational orientation and guidance is to give information on educational and occupational opportunities, and to help the individual to make a choice whose realisation corresponds to his or her aspirations and potential. Thus guidance has to take into account both the individual's qualifications and wishes, society's foreseeable needs and the restrictions on educational capacity.

CHAPTER 8

The content of higher education

One of the most common criticisms with which the idea of manpower planning has to contend is that it pays insufficient attention to the precise content of the knowledge and skills which are implied by the possession of high-level qualifications. The planner's primary variable is indeed qualifications, not education: he or she predicts the need for manpower who have achieved certain educational levels, not, or not directly, those who have acquired certain intellectual and practical capacities. This is not altogether fair criticism. We have seen how planners frequently undertake detailed analyses of jobs and of the skills needed to perform them adequately. But it must be admitted that, as in other areas of planning, more attention is paid to the relatively unproblematic, and measurable, quantitative issues of the size and shape of the higher education system, and far less to the difficult problems concerned with the content of the curriculum.

These problems are indeed difficult. They fall, it seems to us, into two separable areas. One area has to do with the multiple functions which the higher education system performs: as we shall try to show, other functions may be damaged by, or their proponents may resist, an over-emphasis on the manpower requirements of the economy. This problem is a broad social or political one: who, or what needs, should control the content of the curriculum? The other area, however, concerns the equally difficult question of the "right" content of an education for good job performance in a rapidly changing industrial society. Here, too, there is considerable disagreement, and different countries have chosen what appear to be quite sharply different solutions.

The variety of uses to which higher education is put were discussed in Chapter 2. It is clear that the training of qualified manpower is only one of these, and that it may conflict with other demands on the education system. One example of this conflict concerns the content of education directly: namely, the function of social and cultural education, or "education for citizenship" which the education system is also generally expected to carry out. Partly this is a conflict over scarce time or resources. It may take longer to educate a student in the specific vocational skills which he requires, if he must also spend time on other activities which are designed to instil in him a sense of his role in society, and of the purposes to which that society is dedicated. Considerable ingenuity has been demonstrated in some countries in devising methods of teaching and learning which are designed to encourage such values without necessarily reducing the time devoted to the primary technical content of courses. However, the problem may arise more acutely in certain areas of study - perhaps chiefly the social sciences. It has been suggested that one (among many) causes of the student unrest which spread through many universities in the late 1960s was the gap which students perceived between the stated aims of their society and its actual progress in achieving those aims. Thus it is by no means self-evident that an emphasis in the curriculum on social analysis and criticism will automatically lead to better job performance and a cheerful dedication to the goals of society as expressed in practice. On the contrary, it may lead to discontent and, in extreme cases, to an unwillingness to participate in the regular work of what may be defined as a corrupt society.

Another area where conflict might be expected is analogous to the main area of dispute about the uses of manpower planning; that is, the relevance of social demand. It is perhaps curious, however, that student demand does not seem to have any comparable influence on the content of courses in higher education. As we shall suggest, there are other strong forces at work on course content both within universities and colleges, and from outside in the form of demand from the economy. Students, however, are only present in higher education for a short period and cannot, by definition, be expert on the curriculum until they leave. This may partly explain their apparently weak influence. But another factor may be the strength of the over-all demand for places. Probably the biggest leverage which students could exert, especially in the market economies, would be their ability to go elsewhere if their curricular wishes are not met. Where competition by potential students for places is high, and competition by institutions for students scarcely exists, this influence cannot be strong. Nevertheless, it seems likely that the spread of different forms of recurrent education, the increasing age of students (where this is occurring) and the increasing maturity and legal status as adults of young people of student age can, and should, increase their influence on the content of the curriculum.

However, the central dispute over the balance of influences on the curriculum concerns the relative weight of the education and employment systems. Again, the problem is posed in a variety of ways. One form is relatively abstract. There seems to be a potential conflict between the research and knowledge creation function of the education system, and its function in relation to employment. This conflict can be seen in the structural organisation of higher education institutions. As Bergendal (1977) puts it, there is:

> ... a tension inherent in all education, which is reflected in the planning and future organisation of Swedish higher education. The occupational dimension represents an exterior element, whereas the base fields stand for an inner structure of knowledge. The balance between the two dimensions is a vital and controversial point of the planning of all kinds of higher education.

Such a tension cannot, of course, be solved once and for all by any mechanical device of structural rearrangement. Even supposing that good job performance were best served by training students in groups defined by a unique occupational reference (and, as we shall show later, this is by no means self-evident), it would not only be administratively awkward and doubtless costly for universities to do so, but it would cut these groups off from any connection with the progress of knowledge in other related areas. Indeed, it is difficult to imagine what purpose universities would then serve that could not be done equally well by groups of employers. To take a simple example, the teaching of medicine is commonly separated into separate schools for human and animal (veterinary) forms, for a variety of quite sensible reasons, including the obvious differences of some parts of the teaching curriculum, especially its clinical component. Yet a great deal of our knowledge of human physiology and pathology is derived from animal studies. Medical students do not need to talk to veterinary students but professors of medicine must probably talk from time to time, and must certainly exchange papers, with their colleagues in veterinary science.

The problem of balancing the influence of research and employment needs also affects the content of the curriculum more directly. Here, the argument is generally heard as one of "conservatism" versus innovation. Curiously enough, however, the fear of conservatism is adduced as the reason for a wide variety of recommendations. On the one hand, there is a plausible fear that too great a reliance on externally defined vocational education may build in a resistance to innovation. Practising professionals may have too narrow a conception of what is possible, and may wish students to be taught simply the best elements of existing practices. The need to avoid such a possibility is, after all, one of the main reasons why training is done in educational institutions, and not directly by employers. It is important, in other words, that there should be a body of academics, who are not merely teachers but also researchers and thinkers, and who are not confined by the immediate practical demands of production or of earning their own living. Being free from such constraints, these teachers are supposed to develop creative and questioning attitudes of mind, and to pass them on to their students, so that they in turn can transform the methods of the enterprises which they later join as employees. According to this school of thought, employers who complain that graduates lack practical abilities, or fail to fit in easily to their present methods of work, are misunderstanding what universities are capable of doing. If graduates simply fitted neatly into pre-ordained posts, they might just as well have been trained on the job; and in any case it must certainly be the duty of employers to provide them with a certain minimum of specific and practical training.

On the other hand, there is also, so it is said, an inertia or conservatism of academic life. Here there are two somewhat different lines of attack. One argument is simply the converse of that just described. Academics are economically irresponsible in that, unlike professionals, their jobs are not dependent from day to day on their expertise as lawyers or engineers. Thus their teaching can often be irrelevant to the real needs of future employment and it is only the influence of professionals and the demands of employers which bring them back to earth. Indeed, since academic curricula have built into them not only whatever personal conservatism teachers may exhibit but also the inertia of a frequently complex administrative structure, strong pressure is needed from outside universities if new courses are to be developed.

If the problem is posed in these practical terms, it seems that it should be possible to achieve a balance between these two potential focuses of conservatism. Indeed, in many countries (such as Sweden, Romania, and Poland) attempts have been made to involve employers (and governments) more closely in developing courses; to ensure that existing courses are regularly re-examined for their usefulness as well as their relationship to new knowledge; and to ensure as much as possible the interpenetration of education and work, hopefully to the mutual benefit of both.

But the problem of academic inertia can also be posed in rather more sociologically complex terms, which make it seem less easy to resolve. This brings us back to Bergendal's distinction between the structure of knowledge and the structure of occupations. There is a tension, however, between occupational needs and not only the structure of knowledge itself, but also - more importantly - its social organisation. For the academic community is ordered in a complex pattern of interlocking hierarchies, both visible institutions and "invisible colleges" (Crane 1972). To change the content of a course may, in fact, require not so much changing the map of knowledge as changing the location in which it is taught. The internal difficulties of interdisciplinary courses, still more of interdisciplinary departments, are notorious. Thus any attempt such as that in Poland (Kluczynski and Jozefowicz 1977) to recombine university departments and institutes into a smaller number of broader units, though commendable, requires great administrative leverage to make it work effectively. In particular, it may require a new structure of rewards with changed opportunities and criteria for promotion. One of the strongest forces for conservatism in universities may well be their hierarchical structure, whereby in most systems new members of the professoriate are appointed only by existing professors, and in general, the nature of the field is defined and innovation is controlled entirely by those who have benefited from the existing structure.

Nevertheless, innovations do occur. Bergendal (1977) has outlined some instances of interaction between the "pull" of the economy and the "push" from higher education, to create new courses or find new uses for graduates trained in seemingly irrelevant courses. Among the former he includes new courses in Sweden for public administrators, social workers, guidance counsellors and computer programmers and technicians. On the "push" side, the development of the social sciences in the universities has led to the production of graduates in larger numbers than are needed for traditional types of employment. However, some such graduates have begun work on production lines, and have demonstrated to their employers the advantages of their "combination of theoretical training and practical experience" (Bergendal 1977). Thus a supply of graduates with qualifications that had not previously seemed useful has caused employers to create new kinds of jobs. Examples of detailed changes in course content, as opposed to innovations in the provision of courses, are by their nature harder to document. But they undoubtedly occur all the time in response to pressures from both sides.

So far in this chapter we have assumed that the chief difficulty in determining course content lies in the conflicting demands made by different interests, or by different social and economic needs. We have implied, in other words, that both universities and employers believe they know (though they may disagree) what is the appropriate course for a future employee in a given industry. In fact, however, this is a gross over-simplification. For there is considerable disagreement, often on very slender evidence, as to what qualities a graduate brings, or can or should bring, to his or her future employment. Some of this disagreement has been described earlier in our discussion of the issue of "credentialism". Extreme proponents of this view would have us believe that the content of courses is totally irrelevant to job performance, and that all employers either are, or should be, concerned with his success in obtaining a qualification. Evidence which partly confirms this view is provided by surveys of graduates that purport to show how little they have made use of what they learned in higher education. Indeed, the notion of the "substitutability" of highly qualified manpower as a way of adjusting to mismatches gives weight to the argument that course content should not be rigidly tied to the performance of one and only one job. Moreover, the normal expectation of the highly qualified is that they will embark on a complex <u>career</u> involving fairly frequent changes in specific <u>jobs</u>. And even the pace of technological change seems to require that graduates should be adaptable, rather than trained to fit one particular task.

This is indeed the aim of most European planners of higher education. Phrases such as "flexibility" or "adaptability" (in Poland), the encouragement of "independent learning" and "creative thinking and action" (German Democratic Republic) or "permanent self-education" (Hungary) are to be found in most discussions of objectives. "It would be a negation of the necessary for convertibility of knowledge and for comprehensive education if we set, from the beginning, the objectives of a full utilisation, in the job held, of the entire body of knowledge" (Iván 1977). As Hüfner, et al (1977) pointed out, the growth in enrolments also has a tendency to push the education system away from vocationally orientated courses and towards a more general content. This is perhaps especially true in the Federal Republic of Germany: German universities have historically had very strong links between particular faculties and the corresponding professions. These links are weakened by the growth in enrolments, which would inevitably overcrowd the élite professions. At least where growth occurs in relatively undifferentiated courses, there will be strong pressure to make these courses more and more general in their applicability. Nevertheless, there are strong pressures in the opposite direction also. Extreme credentialism, if taken seriously, leads planners to ask whether higher education is not a remarkably costly way of conducting a selection process which could surely be shortened and simplified. In the face of strong social demand, the obvious recourse is not to reduce the provision of higher education but to ensure that higher education is doing more than selection, by increasing its vocational content. This is very often done, not in higher education as a whole, but in the non-university sector (in countries where such a distinction applies). Thus, in the Netherlands, the non-university sector is in fact named "higher vocational education", to distinguish it from the "academic", non-applied content of university education. We suggested earlier (Chapter 2) that a binary system of higher education is a normal response to growth; and this seems to be so in part because there is a limit in any economy to the number of highly qualified by non-vocationally trained manpower that can be absorbed into employment.

There are, however, also pressures - perhaps because of cost considerations - to increase the vocational component of academic, university education. One might well expect these to occur in the centrally planned economies, where manpower planning is used to determine the required numbers both in education and employment. The connection between the two sectors must be reasonably predictable for manpower planning to succeed; and how better to ensure this than by insisting on a substantial vocational component? This has undoubtedly been the case in the past but it is now the market economies which seem to be emphasising vocational content. In the Federal Republic of Germany, the Science Council (Wissenschaftsrat) has called for a greater vocational component in higher education, as has the "U68" Commission in Sweden; while in the Netherlands the authorities are proposing an increasing similarity between the curricula of higher vocational education and the universities. Sweden, at least, is preparing to deal with the problems of substitution and adaptation by increasing enormously the number of short courses, both in-service and for retraining, which will be provided. Meanwhile, Poland and the German Democratic Republic are talking of returning much of the vocational component to employers, and concentrating on education for innovation and creativity. Perhaps the only conclusion to be drawn from this review of factors which should or might influence course content is that there is, as yet, very little certainty in either type of economy as to the appropriate educational content for a wide range of jobs.

CHAPTER 9

The role of lifelong education

This is not the place for an extended discussion of the role of lifelong education in a manpower orientated higher education system. There have in recent years been very many publications on lifelong education and the related concepts of recurrent education, permanent education, continuing education, and so on (see, for example, Williams 1977). However, the acceptance of lifelong education as a practical guiding principle for the further development of educational systems in many countries of the world clearly cannot be ignored by those who are concerned with planning to meet the national needs for highly qualified manpower. There can be little doubt that if opportunities for higher education are genuinely available throughout the lifetime of individuals the task of the manpower planner can become very much easier.

Some of the difficulties confronting those who attempt to base higher education plans on forecasts of qualified manpower needs have been discussed in Chapter 3. In brief, they arise largely from the following factors: the long time horizon necessary; the certainty of unpredictable technological change in any growing economy; the difficulty of establishing an educational system which can provide in detail all the thousands of specific skills that high-level workers require; the limitations on an individual's freedom of occupational choice which can arise if young people are trained for one and only one specific job; and the problem of ensuring a smooth path of development for higher education, while at the same time overcoming specific high-level manpower shortages as quickly as possible. To be able to distribute higher education opportunities throughout the lifetime of individuals instead of concentrating them prior to entry into the labour force can make a substantial contribution to the solution of all these problems. It can also contribute to an improvement of the relationships between the content of higher education and the needs of the world of work. In the remainder of this chapter we consider each of these six issues in turn.

Length of planning period

There are really two aspects of this problem. One of the reasons why there are difficulties in adjusting the output of the higher education system to meet the needs of employment is that, under traditional arrangements for higher education, graduates are in employment for a period of 40 years or more after they have completed their higher education. Thus, in principle at least, any manpower forecasting exercise ought to look at the total lifetime career prospects available for various kinds of specialists, and not just at their prospects at the point of entry into the labour force. This is particularly important in occupations with rigid hierarchical career structures. If a period of rapid growth of a particular occupational category is followed by much slower growth, serious promotion bottlenecks will result: either the proportion of workers who can expect promotion to the senior grades must decline, or the average age at which they expect promotion must rise. Either event would normally be considered a deterioration of career prospects. One effect of the explosive expansion of higher education during the 1960s was to create just such promotion bottlenecks in universities and colleges. The second reason why a long time horizon is necessary in manpower planning is that if higher education is to provide young people with all the skills and knowledge they may need throughout their working lives the length of initial training must be fairly long. Four years is in practice about the minimum; in the Netherlands it is normally seven to eight years. To this time period required for actual training must be added the length of time necessary before planning decisions can be made effective. This period is often another two or three years in decentralised systems such as that of the Federal Republic of Germany. Thus as much as ten years may elapse before a decision by planners to change the output of particular types of graduates can have any substantial effect upon the numbers entering the labour force with that particular qualification.

A system of lifelong opportunities for higher education can help to alleviate both of these problems.

Essentially, it does so by introducing a greater degree of flexibility into the education-employment relationship. Let us take a theoretical example. Under traditional arrangements, four years of higher education may be expected to last an individual for 40 years of working life. Leaving aside the problems of technological change and the depreciation and obsolescence of skills, which are dealt with below, each year of higher education would then provide training for ten years of working life. In order to make a fully successful manpower plan in such a system a planner would need to have some broad perspective for the 40 years that graduates will be in the labour force, and to allow for a period of at least six years before decisions taken now can have an effect on the number of newly qualified workers entering the labour force. Let us suppose that this is replaced by a system in which each individual has the opportunity of six months of full-time higher education every five years or so. In this case the length of working life which would need to be covered by each dose of education would be five rather than 40 years and it would be between six months and a year before planning decisions could be made effective rather than six years or more.

Of course, in practice there are likely to be many complexities. Certainly an initial period of higher education longer than six months would almost certainly be necessary. Furthermore, there are likely to be many interdependencies between previous work experience, ability to absorb new kinds of higher education and new career prospects. However, the principle that lifelong learning opportunities can reduce very considerably the time horizon over which detailed manpower forecasts need to be made is a very important one, in practice as well as in theory.

Specificity of skills

In any dynamic modern economy many thousands of specific skills are required in the labour force and these are constantly changing. It is quite impossible to expect the educational system to provide young people with all the skills that they will require throughout their working lives. The role of education, including higher education, should be to provide young people with the intellectual equipment to be able to learn the specific skills which are required in the kind of employment they enter. This is not an argument against all specialisation in higher education. To some degree it makes sense to group different kinds of skills together. For example, some occupations require the ability to manipulate quantitative data; others require the ability to write convincing and persuasive reports and so on. We have seen in Chapter 8 how basic fields of study can be related to occupational training sectors. However, this can be done only at a fairly high level of aggregation. In any higher education system which aims to meet specific manpower needs there will be constant pressure from employers for the content of higher education to be more and more job specific. This will enable graduates to take up particular occupations at less cost in initial training to employers; but it will also make it less easy for them to acquire other skills, or to change their jobs as their careers develop. Lifelong education provides a way out of this dilemma.

The ideal curriculum in a system of lifelong education might enable students to acquire a combination of very generalised transferable skills (such as the ability to communicate in one or more languages, or a thorough knowledge of fundamental mathematical ideas) together with the very specific skills required by the student for the particular occupation he intends to take up when he first enters the labour force. These would presumably be mainly vocational but could also include those civic skills, in the case of high-level manpower, necessary to function as a community leader. More and more modules of specific knowledge could then be added throughout the individual's life as he had need of them. Once again the implication for manpower planning is that it would lessen the need for detailed and rigid long-term plans.

The problem of technological change

When the concept of lifelong education started to be taken seriously during the 1960s one of the main motive forces was the growing realisation that in many technical and applied scientific professions, such as engineering, medicine and agriculture, technological change was becoming so rapid that a single "dose" of education early in life was no longer sufficient to last people throughout their working life. Their knowledge became obsolete long before they reached retirement. The result was not only economic inefficiency but also all kinds of psychological tensions within individuals and between individuals, especially between older and younger professional workers.

This need for updating of skills brought about by technological change led to the rapid development in many countries of post-experience higher education. This has been the subject of a useful series of studies by the International Institute for Educational Planning. The studies revealed that there has been a considerable development in post-experience higher education in many countries, especially in the area of management education. This expansion has been partly the result of "growing demand from governments, industry, agriculture and other branches of activity as well as from specialists and former graduates of higher education who wish to improve their qualifications, update or retrain" (Onushkin 1974).

Stoikov (1973) has pointed out that there are two different processes which result in the need for refreshment of the skills and abilities of individual workers. "There is the physical deterioration of the individual and the deterioration of his skills and knowledge. These two are not necessarily related."

Physical deterioration which in most cases can simply be equated with forgetting things which were learned a long time ago, provides an obvious need for retraining where an individual is going to take on new occupational responsibilities. As people get older they forget things they have learned and lose the ability to absorb new information, unless they have the opportunity of using their knowledge and exercising their learning skills from time to time. Thus, even if there were no technological change, there would still be an important role for higher education in providing retraining facilities for adults at various stages in their working lives. The risk of such forgetfulness is particularly strong when human capital is not put to use for some time, as in the case of workers who are subject to long periods of unemployment. The problem may be particularly serious for highly qualified women who subsequently spend several years outside the labour force bringing up their children.

Deterioration of skills and knowledge occurs for several reasons and in several different ways. Many jobs, even highly skilled ones, require long periods of routine work which can result in staleness. Workers develop automatic behaviour responses that inhibit them from responding to changes when they do occur. In jobs where sudden emergencies occur, or where high levels of attention and ability are required intermittently, the consequences of such deterioration may be serious. In addition to the more dramatic aspects of the problem, workers with specialised skills often find themselves in work situations where they are isolated from other workers with similar skills. Opportunity for discussion with other specialists can be a valuable educational experience, giving new interest to the job and enhancing efficiency.

However, a more important type of deterioration of skills is that brought about not by changes in the mental abilities of the individual worker but by new scientific discoveries and changes in technology. People affected by such changes need to have their knowledge and skills updated from time to time if they are to continue to make their full contribution to the economy and to society. If opportunities for such updating and refreshment of knowledge and skills are freely available, planners are again freed from the necessity to attempt the impossible task of making detailed forecasts of technological change.

Limitation on freedom of occupational choice

The more specific is the initial vocational training received by students, the less choice of occupation do they have when they come to enter the labour force. This is not intrinsically bad. Someone who has acquired skills which will enable him to enter a well-paid job with high social status and prestige is unlikely to feel encumbered by this limitation on his freedom of choice. However, not all individuals will have been so lucky. For many, a lifelong restriction of job opportunities based entirely on academic performance during a period of higher education before entry to the labour force, will appear as a very considerable burden. Nevertheless, this is one of the possible implications of detailed manpower planning of traditional higher education. Lifelong education offers a way out of this straitjacket: but it also has dangers.

One of the most delicate issues in lifelong education is that of educational credentials. Credentialism, referring to the collection by students of possibly irrelevant certificates of educational attainment in order to impress employers, has in recent years been the subject of much criticism (e.g. Dore, 1976).

The alleged evils of credentialism are, first, that those who obtain paper qualifications are believed to be favoured in recruitment to certain jobs at the expense of equally able people without formal qualifications; secondly, that the pursuit of these pieces of paper by individuals wishing to obtain such discrimination in their favour results in a depreciation of the value of qualifications; and, thirdly, that a preoccupation with examinations and assessment distorts the purposes and processes of education. The first of these criticisms must by definition be true of any system of higher education based upon manpower planning unless it is accompanied by an ideal system of initial selection. There is little evidence that such an ideal system of selection has yet been developed.

In many countries the expansion of higher education in the 1960s led to a situation in which educational credentials were deemed necessary prerequisites for entry to jobs where the formal educational experience which led to the qualification was not strictly necessary for the successful performance of the jobs. It is indeed very convenient for employers to be able to use educational qualifications as a preliminary screening device in selecting recruits. It is a practice that has much to recommend it. It can limit the advantages of rich and powerful persons by curbing (but unfortunately not entirely removing) their ability to use their wealth, influence and access to information to secure employment advantages for themselves and for their children. Furthermore, since passing examinations normally required a certain amount of ability and hard work, the use of educational credentials as criteria of eligibility for high-level jobs eliminates those who have little ability or who are irretrievably lazy. However, it also eliminates many people who, for financial or social reasons, or because they were badly advised or merely unlucky at critical points in their educational career, were not able to obtain the requisite qualifications.

One of the main aims of lifelong education is to provide a network of flexible educational and career options. It would be ironic indeed if lifelong education itself, by providing credentials, restricted opportunities for career advancement to people who have had particular educational experiences. It would be a perversion of the aims of lifelong education if its spread turns out to mean that evaluation not only of an individual's suitability for initial recruitment but also his fitness for promotion in his career is determined largely on the basis of formally acquired educational qualifications. However, it is unrealistic to assume that the full benefit of lifelong higher education can be obtained without the award of certificates of competence to those students who successfully undertake courses of retraining. The important point is to ensure that opportunities to obtain the qualifications are as open as possible; and that students are not precluded for unjustifiable reasons from undertaking courses that will enable them to further their careers.

It is also important - and this must be a particular responsibility of manpower planners - that workers who have successfully undertaken courses should be able to find jobs that are commensurate with their new levels of competence. Provided that these safeguards are observed, the existence of continuing educational opportunities throughout life will lessen any sense of grievance that an individual worker may feel if his initial qualifications do not enable him to obtain the job that he would really like.

Stable paths of higher education expansion

In all the countries which make extensive use of manpower planning, considerable importance is attached to the securing of stable paths of growth in higher education, even where the rate of growth of required manpower stocks is somewhat erratic. The essence of the problem is the simple mathematical relationship between stocks and flows. If attempts are made rapidly to overcome a shortage of particular kinds of qualified manpower through increasing the number of new entrants to the labour force, this will require a level of enrolments in higher education that is not sustainable in the long run when the initial manpower shortage has been overcome. Two kinds of difficulties can follow from the resulting fluctuation. One is over-capacity of teachers and equipment in certain branches of higher education. The other is a sense of unfairness amongst new generations of potential students, in that the breadth of higher education opportunities open to them is less than that available to their predecessors. Such fluctuations can also lead to imbalances and promotion bottlenecks in the stock of qualified manpower. If shortages of qualified manpower can be overcome by upgrading the existing manpower stock through short courses of retraining, both the potential excess capacity and the sense of lost opportunity will be very much reduced.

The content of higher education and the needs of the world of work

We have seen in Chapter 8 that unless steps are taken to counter them there are strong tendencies for the content of higher education to be determined by academic criteria, the needs of the discipline, rather than by the needs of the economy and society. A system of higher education based upon lifelong education, in which a majority of the students have already had substantial experience of the world of work is far more likely to be under pressure from its students to offer courses which are relevant to economic needs. The authority of teachers in such a system will depend not upon their greater age and experience but upon whether they have something to teach which the adult students wish to learn. This point has been made very forcibly in a study of the relations between higher education and manpower planning in Sweden:

> When the wisdom of adding one three-year cycle to another in education has been questioned, one of the major points of criticism is that the contacts between the studies and the world of work are getting too weak. Young people of the age of 25, who have not yet had full job responsibility, run too great a risk to be alienated to society and its requirements. Also, a meritocracy is being developed in which a certain formal education is considered necessary for a job even in

cases where practical experience would be as good or better a background ... Early periods of work will allow young people to test their abilities so as to give a good background for the choice of future activities. The young may want to go on in the field of their first choice, using on-the-job training or formalised studies that can be highly specialised or very general. They may also want to change their field of activity. In either case, the experiences, skills, knowledge, and attitudes gained in work will most probably be an asset in the future, for both the individual and his work, Bergendal (1977).

In summary there can be little doubt that in both the formulation and implementation of manpower based plans for higher education in their quantitative and qualitative aspects, the development of lifelong education provides unprecedented opportunities for the harmonisation of the demands of individual students with the general needs of society for qualified manpower. Bergendal (1977) concludes:

Is it realistic to think that recurrent education, and the policy measures connected with it within the areas of both education and work, will reconcile individual and social aspects? Can planning based on individual preferences also meet the needs of society? Even if it is probably unrealistic to believe in total harmony with no conflicts between the various interests involved, it seems that recurrent education will give some hope of improvement ...

The established policy of educational planning has stressed generality and the postponement of occupational specialisation. Recurrent education offers an alternative in which breadth is accomplished not essentially by the generality of abstract studies, but by the varied experiences over a broad field of human activities. It may then be an advantage to introduce some specialisation fairly early, not as a decisive step to produce a narrow specialist for life, but as an element of a broad individual pattern of experiences.

The full implications of recurrent education are not only to improve possibilities to make education meet the demands of the economy. At least as essential is the possible strong influence of education and science on the development of the economy and on society as a whole.

CHAPTER 10

Woman power

In Chapter 1 we illustrated the well-known fact that one of the experiences common to every European country in the post-War period was a marked expansion of higher education. Another general phenomenon has been the increased participation of females. It is not our purpose here to discuss the complex phenomena which underlie this trend, except in so far as they concern planners of manpower needs and of higher education. It is useful, however, to indicate the extent of change since 1950 in the seven European countries under consideration: these changes are summarised in table 10.1.

Table 10.1: Percentage of students in third-level education who are female

	1950	1955	1960	1965	1970	1974
Germany, Fed. Rep.	19	19	23	24	26	34*
Germany, Dem. Rep.	23	29	32	28	43	52
Hungary		24	33	39	43	47
Netherlands	21	25	26	25	28	31
Poland	36	36	41	46	47	53
Romania	33	35	33	39	43	44
Sweden	23	29	33	41	42	46

* 1975 figure.

Source: UNESCO (1965); UNESCO (1975); UNESCO (1977).

The figures in table 10.1 are derived from reports to UNESCO. We must again warn against placing too much emphasis on international comparisons, since the types of institution include under "third-level" education can vary from country to country or even from year to year within one country. Nevertheless, certain tentative comparisons may be legitimate. Primarily, however, the table shows a steady increase in every country in the proportion of students who are women. At one extreme, in the Netherlands women have increased from 21 per cent to 31 per cent as a proportion of the student body; at the other, in the German Democratic Republic they have increased from 23 per cent to 52 per cent. In almost every country the rate of change has been fairly steady throughout the 25-year period. Indeed, in some countries the two factors of population growth and increased female participation in higher education go far towards accounting for the increase in social demand.

Despite our reservations about international comparisons, it is hard to escape the observation that the centrally planned economies and Sweden have been considerably more successful than the Netherlands and the Federal Republic of Germany in increasing female participation, and indeed in reducing sex differences to a minimum. In the former five countries, women now constitute nearly half of all third-level students (more than half in the case of Poland and the German Democratic Republic); whereas in the Netherlands and the Federal Republic, the proportion is approximately one-third. However, in the early 1950s we should not have grouped the countries in the same way: at that time Poland and Romania had high levels of female participation (at around one-third of all students) compared with the five other countries, each with a little less than one-quarter. It may be tempting to jump to conclusions about the reasons for these differences. Before doing so, however, we must look more closely at female participation, since the figures given in table 10.1 inevitably conceal considerable internal variation.

There is, for example, considerable variation between one sector of higher education and another, as table 10.2 shows. It describes female enrolment rates in subdivisions of the total higher education system. Inevitably, the categories vary from country to country: but the table shows, first, that universities tend to have a smaller proportion of women students than some other sectors of higher education, especially teacher training; and secondly, that women are, or have been likely to enrol at a higher rate in intra-mural, full-time courses than in extra-mural courses. (This statement is markedly true of the German Democratic Republic; it has also applied to Hungary and Romania until very recently.) Women's lower enrolment in universities is partly explained by sharp differences in subject preferences between the two sexes, which we discuss below: but it is clear that, at least in the market economies, girls also have somewhat lower ambitions than boys at the point of choice of higher education institution. This can be illustrated by the transition rates with Ritzen (1977) reports. According to the most recent figures for the Netherlands, almost 100 per cent of boys graduating from the <u>gymnasium</u> (selective academic secondary school) enter university, compared with roughly 80 per cent and 90 per cent of girls from its two streams. The remainder of the girls choose to attend higher vocational education (which includes teacher training institutions). From the two streams of HBS (a more vocational secondary school, but with pre-university curricula - now superseded) transition rates to university in 1971 were: boys, 60 per cent and 80 per cent; girls, 30 per cent and 60 per cent. Girls have until recently had higher transition rates from such "pre-university" schools to higher vocational education; however, girls have been less inclined than boys to transfer to this sector of higher education from vocational secondary schools. Part of the problem, therefore, appears to be that girls with equivalent qualifications have lower aspirations and are either less willing or less able to enter higher education at any level. It should be added, however, that girls' transition rates, like boys', have been rising steadily for many years. Boys from selective secondary schools now seem to be close to the natural limit of almost universal transfer to higher education; girls' transfer rates are expected by Dutch planners to continue to rise.

Table 10.2   PERCENTAGE OF STUDENTS WHO ARE FEMALE, BY SECTOR OF HIGHER EDUCATION

	UNESCO: 1974/75 TOTAL 3RD LEVEL								
FRG 1975/76	34	Universities/ Tech. Univs 32	Teacher Colleges 65	Colleges of Arts, Music etc. 41	Technical Colleges 23	Comprehensive Academies 31			
					Colleges (inc. Teacher Training)				
GDR 1974	52	Universities Intra-mural 56 Extra-mural 20 ⎱ 49			Intra-mural 72 Extra-mural 48 ⎱ 59				
Hungary 1974	47	Intra-mural 48	Extra-mural 46						
Netherlands 1974	31	Universities 25 (New admissions 1976) (31)			Higher vocational education (inc. teacher training) 37				
Poland 1974/75	53	Universities: faculties range from 42% (law and administration) to 74% (arts)	Teacher training academies 71	Medical academies 64	Economics High Schools 65	Fine Arts High Schools 49	Rural Science Academies 44	Polytechnics 24
Romania 1974/75	44	Full-time intra-mural 47		Evening 24	Correspondence 45				
Sweden	46								

- 116 -

In Sweden, transfer rates direct from school are higher for girls than for boys, owing to the intervention of national service for males; but transition rates within the first four years after leaving school are substantially higher for males: the four-year rate for boys from the _gymnasium_ was roughly 90 per cent for those leaving school in 1969, compared with roughly 70 per cent for girls. Unlike the Netherlands, where girls' transfer rates are still rising, the recent decline in transfer rates in Sweden seems to have applied to both sexes. It appears that the near-equality of the sexes in present-day Swedish higher education (see table 10.1) results not from equal aspirations among school-leavers, but from a larger enrolment of women at a later stage in their lives.

Several different factors must combine to cause the internal differences in female participation found in table 10.2. First, data on transition rates from the Netherlands and Sweden strongly suggest a pattern of lower aspirations by female school-leavers, even among those with the highest secondary school qualifications. Whether such differences in aspiration are still present among girls in the centrally planned economies - as they undoubtedly were 20 years ago - is not entirely clear from the data available to us. Since in these countries women's participation is roughly equal to men's in higher education as a whole, and indeed is higher than men's in several countries on intra-mural courses (which have the highest recruitment of school-leavers), we suspect that the problem of lower aspirations does not exist to the same extent. But it is clear from the figures already given that women's enrolment is always higher in colleges or in courses providing training for teaching, than it is on the more academic courses in universities. This forms part of a pattern of self-selection by the sexes into different fields of study, and it is to this pattern that we now turn.

Table 10.3: Percentage of students in third level education who are female by discipline: latest year available

	(Year)	Education	Medical subjects	Humanities	Social science	Natural science	Engineering
Germany Fed. Rep.	(1971)	60	26	47	23	20	2
Germany Dem. Rep.	(1973)	78	72	52	62	42	23
Hungary	(1973)	81	56	69	60	52	20
Netherlands	(1971)	46	22	42	26	15	7
Poland	(1973)	66	77	72	65	64	25
Romania	(1973)	56	66	73	50	56	27
Sweden	(1973)	77	59	61	40	24	9

Source: Computed from UNESCO (1975): table 5.2.

Table 10.3 gives, from figures reported to UNESCO, the proportion of women in most of the major subject groupings of third-level education. There are interesting similarities, and also differences, between the various countries. On the one hand, education recruits the highest proportion of women in five out of the seven countries; the humanities, too, always have a higher proportion of women than does the higher education system as a whole. And engineering subjects consistently have a low proportion of women - strikingly low in the three market economies. Research suggests that a combination of influences is at work here. It has been traditional in most societies for girls of secondary school age to tend to concentrate on the arts and literature, while boys of the same age specialise more often in mathematics and the quantitative disciplines. It is possible to see the influence of such patterns in these figures for higher education, at least as far as relative preferences for the humanities and engineering subjects are concerned. But the position of the natural sciences in table 10.2 warns us that early subject preferences cannot be a complete explanation. For in three of the centrally planned economies (Hungary, Poland and Romania) the proportion of women in the natural science faculties is higher than their proportion in higher education as a whole - and in the case of Poland and Romania, there are, relatively, about as many women students in sciences as there are in education. An alternative explanation is suggested by the fact that the largest differences are, in most countries, between engineering and education. These are both vocationally specific subjects. The teaching profession has traditionally been particularly favoured by and welcoming to women, whereas careers in engineering have, in the market economies at least, been regarded as almost ludicrously unsuitable. The latter is perhaps a stereotyped view. In modern industry there are surely many careers in technology which are no more physically demanding than a whole range of while-collar jobs; and indeed the number of women enrolling in these subjects at universities and colleges is slowly increasing in most countries. But Pestisanu, et al (1977) points out that there are still jobs in this area which women may plausibly avoid because of their physical demands, such as mining, metallurgy, geology and petroleum exploration. Education, on the other hand, is probably attractive to women, not because of its light physical demands (which can be quite severe in practice) but because of its social organisation. One of its obvious conveniences is that teachers can be reasonably confident of arriving home at the same time as their children. School teaching requires comparatively few hours to be spent at the place of work, and it can fairly easily be organised to allow for part-time employment. It is also a profession in which it is possible to re-enter employment after a period of absence. All of these features have advantages for the conventional family arrangement in which the mother takes the major responsibility for the early years of child rearing. Indeed, some market economies have tended to regard married women as a kind of reserve army of potential school teachers, to be called on temporarily in case of a shortage of supply. Finally, for some women school teaching, especially in primary schools where the percentage of women teachers is highest, is socially and psychologically attractive, since it can be defined as an extension of the family role of motherhood. In societies where women's participation in employment has been seen as socially ambiguous or even undesirable, school teaching, like nursing, seems to be one of the more generally acceptable jobs for women.

The cases of the natural sciences and medicine are more complicated. The figures of table 10.3 still conceal a great deal of internal variation (for example "medical subjects" probably include nursing in some but not all countries). But it appears that the centrally planned economies enrol far higher percentages of women into courses in both of these areas than do the market economies - with the exception of Sweden, where the percentage of women in medicine is also high. This difference probably accounts for much of the higher representation of women in higher education as a whole in these countries. As Iván (1977) points out, when women are concentrated in a few areas and excluded (by their own choice or otherwise) from the full range of subjects, the effect is to make competition for admissions to higher education more severe for women than for men. This may be one reason why their enrolment is lower in the Federal Republic of Germany and the Netherlands.

It is not easy to discover the reasons which lie behind the increased participation of women in the centrally planned economies - or the relatively low rates in the market economies. Among other factors, it may be important that concern in the centrally planned economies has extended beyond enrolling women in higher education to ensuring their participation in greater proportions in the labour force. Figures provided by Sachse (1977) for the German Democratic Republic demonstrate the effects on employment: the proportion of university graduates employed in the labour force who are women has risen from 24 per cent in 1961 to 30 per cent in 1974, while the proportion among college graduates has risen over the same period from 32 per cent to 43 per cent. (Even so, women are a much smaller proportion of employed graduates than they are of the total labour force, of which 47 per cent were women in 1965.) Similarly in Romania, the proportion of all employed graduates who are women has risen from 30 per cent in 1958 to 35 per cent in 1968.

From a manpower planning point of view, it is obviously economically wasteful to encourage women to enrol in higher education if they are then unavailable for employment. In Sweden, the two sexes have now reached near equality in their rates of taking up paid employment after graduation, having converged from a position of substantial difference even in the late 1960s. In the Netherlands, too, there are no appreciable differences between the employment rates of unmarried women graduates and male graduates, but married women have lower employment rates, and women with children lower still. This may not be entirely due to voluntary withdrawal from employment: it seems that in the market economies married women, especially with children, are at a considerable disadvantage in competing for scarce jobs in a crowded labour market, Ritzen (1977). Thus higher education may reasonably seem an uncertain economic investment for women who intend to have a family. In centrally planned economies with the supply of and demand for qualified personnel better balanced, women need not be discouraged from entering higher education by doubts about their long-term employability; and this may provide them with an extra incentive to enrol. But it is clear, in addition, that the centrally planned economies have placed considerable stress on increasing the participation of women, as part of a general emphasis on increasing social equality and the democratisation of access to higher education. Although their attempts in this direction have apparently not included specific quotas or any manipulation of entrance requirements, they have demonstrated a higher degree of concern than most market economies, which have so far been content with eliminating overt discrimination against women in the education systems. One factor that is certainly important is that higher proportions of women as a whole, qualified and unqualified, are employed in the centrally planned economies, which provide greater social and practical support to working women, including the mothers of young children. Women graduates no longer need to claim special consideration as the possessors of scarce talents. In the market economies, greater social support at least seems to be forthcoming in recent years; and this may underlie the steady increases in higher education enrolments by young women.

It is, of course, always easier to encourage new groups of entrants when the demand for highly qualified manpower is high. In the era of over-supply which the market economies have now entered, it may be politically difficult to provide extra incentives for women. But it is clear that in the market economies sex differences still conceal at least as large a reservoir of talent as do social class differences. The difference between the two is that, to judge by the persistent growth in female enrolment rates in these countries, women are likely to exert continual pressure on higher education and the labour market for some time to come.

CHAPTER 11

An appraisal of the current situation

In this study we have considered the approaches of a number of centrally planned and market economies in Europe to the problem of relating the provision of higher education to the economic and social needs of the nation. Broadly speaking, we have found that in the planned economies - at least as represented by the German Democratic Republic, Hungary, Poland and Romania - the basic criterion determining the size and structure of higher education is the expected needs of the economy for specific categories of qualified manpower. However, this manpower planning criterion is tempered to some extent by the two alternative aims of encouraging an orientation towards social equality in the provision of higher education and of allowing a measure of individual choice. Examples of the former are the special encouragement given in some countries to young people from workers' homes and from rural areas who apply for entry to higher education. Individual freedom of choice is usually permitted within the constraints of manpower plans. Thus the number of places in most university faculties is determined by forecast manpower needs whereas the admission of any particular student is determined by the preference of the students, often after consultation with counsellors, and competitive entrance examinations, modified somewhat by the equality considerations mentioned above.

In those economies that place greater reliance on the operation of the market for the allocation of economic resources, represented in this study by the Federal Republic of Germany, the Netherlands and Sweden, the starting point in planning the future size and structure of higher education is the expected demand for places by individual school-leavers and, increasingly, other adults who missed the opportunity of higher education when they were younger or who wish to upgrade their qualifications. This basic criterion, however, of planning on the basis of social demand is also somewhat modified in practice, to take account of manpower needs in particular areas - of which medical doctors and school teachers are the most common examples. Although the establishment of greater social equality was one of the underlying forces fuelling the rapid expansion of higher education in these countries during the 1960s, there have been few specific policy measures to promote such equality with the exception in some countries of differential financial grants which favour students from poorer families. It should be pointed out also that although the provision of higher education has been based on social demand it has not been provided for all individuals who sought it. In all countries there is a qualifying examination which sometimes takes on the nature of a competitive entrance examination.

Thus, although the approach to planning higher education provision has two very different starting points in the planned and the market economies of Europe, in practice the gap between the two groups is not nearly so wide. In both, moreover, the outcome of these different approaches was a very rapid growth of enrolment during the 1960s succeeded apparently by rather slower growth from the early 1970s onwards.

Recent developments suggest that there may be even more convergence between the two groups of countries. On the one hand, many countries in Western Europe are beginning to be troubled by the emergence of significant amounts of unemployment amongst qualified workers for the first time since the 1930s; on the other, there are some signs that for the first time since the Second World War the demand for higher education by individuals in the planned economies may be growing more rapidly than the number of places needed to meet forecast manpower needs. Although these difficulties have not yet reached serious dimensions in either group of countries, the underlying problem of the gap between what individual students would like and what is socially and economically possible is reaching the stage on both sides where a reappraisal of existing practices seems justified.

It is tempting to seek to evaluate the two contrasting approaches to planning higher education provision by comparing forecasts made in the various countries some years ago with the actual outcome in terms of enrolments and employment patterns some years later.

As we have seen in Chapter 3, many of the critics of manpower planning claim that the long-term forecasts necessary for educational planning are impossible to make in a dynamic economy. Such critics back their claims with examples which show how the actual employment of qualified manpower has differed from that forecast. (See, for example, Ahamad and Blaug, 1973). In the present study, we do not have the statistical information to permit such an approach which is not likely to be very conclusive in any case. If the aim of a forecast is to provide rigid guidelines for the education and manpower system any forecast is likely to prove to be correct, since decisions will be taken to ensure that it is fulfilled. If, on the other hand, manpower forecasts are made but essential decisions about enrolments are based on the social demand for places it will be quite exceptional for the outcome to match the forecasts. Certainly, if economies behaved in accordance with the rigid version of the manpower hypothesis which excludes the possibilities of substitution, any surplus graduates in any area would be unemployed, while shortages of manpower could remain in other areas. However, most practitioners argue that some substitution can occur, particularly in the medium and long term. A more meaningful question is to ask how much economic and social waste is incurred in not meeting planned targets, as compared with what would have occurred if the manpower structure of the plan had been met; but this is the kind of question to which an empirical answer is almost impossible.

The most realistic test is whether manpower forecasts result in better decisions about the provision of higher education than would alternative criteria. The main alternative criterion is social (or individual) demand for places. In the market economies neither social demand nor manpower forecasts have performed at all well as a basis for predicting future developments that determine the provision of higher education (see, for example, Ahamad and Blaug, 1973; Layard, King and Moser, 1969; and OECD, 1971). This suggests that in such economies neither the actions of employers nor those of students are easy to predict. In planned economies, on the other hand, there is quite naturally a much closer correspondence between planning targets, however formulated, and actual outcomes. But this is inherent in the systems of planning and control, and not in the techniques of projections and forecasting.

What does emerge from this study is that any country which wishes to use manpower forecasts as the main basis for planning higher education needs to devote considerable resources to the activity both in formulating the plan and in implementing it. Manpower planning requires substantial activities in the central planning agencies, in the universities and other institutions of higher education and in the main employing enterprises.

The final question that may be asked is whether manpower planning is likely to prove more successful in planned economies than in market economies. The answer to that question is obviously yes. Presumably any type of planning is likely to be more successful in economies where the main resource allocation decisions are taken according to planned social priorities than in economies where the main decisions are taken as the result of market transactions.

What is needed in both types of economy is a model of the higher education system, and the interactions between it and the rest of society, which enable the outcomes of a variety of different policies to be tested. The difference between the countries examined in this report is not so much whether higher education developments are based on manpower considerations or not, as whether they are planned at all or not. In the 1970s we are discovering that unplanned expansion can lead to all sorts of social and economic imbalances; while too rigid planning can result in excessive limitation on individual choice. However, much of the social and economic values underlying the use of these techniques continue to differ, there are increasing pressures leading to a convergence of the technical aspects of alternative planning approaches.

References I - The country case studies

G. Bergendal: Higher Education and Manpower Planning in Sweden (Geneva/Bucharest, ILO/CEPES, 1977).

K. Hüfner, H. Köhler and J. Naumann: Higher Education and Manpower Planning in the Federal Republic of Germany (Geneva/Bucharest, ILO/CEPES, 1977).

A. P. Iván: Higher Education and Manpower Planning in Hungary (Geneva/Bucharest, ILO/CEPES, 1977).

J. Kluczyński and A. Józefowicz: Higher Education and Manpower Planning in Poland (Geneva/Bucharest, ILO/CEPES, 1977).

C. Pestisanu, D.F. Lazaroiu and P. Burloiu: L'enseignement Supérieur et la Planification de la Main-d'Oeuvre dans la République Socialiste de Roumanie (Geneva/Bucharest, ILO/CEPES, 1977).

J.M.M. Ritzen: Higher Education and Manpower Planning in the Netherlands (Geneva/Bucharest, ILO/CEPES, 1977).

E. Sachse: Higher Education and Manpower Planning in the German Democratic Republic (Geneva/Bucharest, ILO/CEPES, 1977).

References II - Other studies

B. Ahamad and M. Blaug, eds.: The Practice of Manpower Forecasting (Amsterdam, Elsevier, 1973).

M. Blaug: An Introduction to the Economics of Education (Harmondsworth, Allen Lane, The Penguin Press, 1970).

D. Crane: Invisible Colleges: Diffusion of Knowledge in Scientific Communities (Chicago, University of Chicago Press, 1972).

S-O Döös: "Long-term employment forecasting: some problems with special reference to current organisation and method in Sweden", in Employment Forecasting (Paris, OECD, 1963).

R. Dore: The Diploma Disease (London, Unwin Education Books, 1976).

F. Edding: Internationale Tendenzen in der Entwicklung der Ausgaben für Schulen und Hochschulen (Kiel, Institut für Weltwirtschaft, 1958).

J. Fourastié: "Employment forecasting in France", in Employment Forecasting - Report of an International Seminar on Employment Forecasting Techniques (Paris, OECD, 1962).

R.B. Freeman: The Market for College-Trained Manpower: A Study in the Economics of Career Choice (Cambridge (Mass.), Harvard University Press, 1971).

H. Goldstein and S. Swerdloff: Methods of Long-term Projection of Requirements for and Supply of Qualified Manpower (Paris, UNESCO, 1967).

H. den Hartog and B.A. Thoolen: Requirements and Supply of Qualified Manpower - Projections for the Netherlands (Amsterdam, Central Planning Office, 1971; Occasional Paper No. 2).

R.G. Hollister: "Economics of Manpower Forecasting", in International Labour Review (Geneva, ILO), April 1964.

R.G. Hollister: "A Technical Evaluation of the OECD's Mediterranean Regional Project: Methods and Conclusions", in G.Z. Bereday, J.A. Lauwerys and M. Blaug, eds.: World Yearbook of Education 1967, Educational Planning (London, Evans, 1967).

C. Jencks, et al: Inequality: A Reassessment of the Effect of Family and Schooling in America (New York, Basic Books Inc., 1972).

E.J. King, C. Moor and J. Mundy: Post-Compulsory Education: A New Analysis in Western Europe (London, Sage, 1974).

Kultusministerkonferenz (KMK): Bedarfsfeststellung 1961 bis 1970 (Stuttgart, Klett, 1965).

G. Krijnen: Ontwikkeling Functievervulling van Psychologen (Nijmegen, ITS, 1976).

P.B.M. de Laat: De Arbeidssituatie voor Fysic: Resultaten van een Delphionderzoek naar vraag, aanbod en overschot in 1980 en 1990 (Utrecht, Stichting FCM, 1975).

P.R.G. Layard and J.C. Saigal: "Educational and occupational characteristics of manpower: an international comparison", in British Journal of Industrial Relations, July 1966.

R. Layard, J. King and C. Moser: The Impact of Robbins (Harmondsworth, Penguin, 1969).

C.E.V. Leser: Can Economists Foretell the Future? (Leeds, University Press, 1969).

E. Mansfield: Industrial Research and Technological Innovation (New York, Norton and Co., Inc., 1968).

A. Maslow: The Farther Reaches of Human Nature (Harmondsworth, Penguin, 1973).

C.A. Moser and R. Layard: "Estimating the need for qualified manpower in Britain", in M. Blaug: Economics of Education: Selected Readings, Vol. 1 (Harmondsworth, Penguin, 1968).

M. O'Donoghue: Economic Dimensions in Education (Dublin, Gill and Macmillan, 1971).

OECD: The Mediterranean Regional Project: An Experiment in Planning by Six Countries (Paris, OECD, 1965).

OECD: Methods and Statistical Needs for Educational Planning (Paris, OECD, 1967).

OECD: Occupational and Educational Structures of the Labour Force and Levels of Economic Development: Possibilities and Limitations of an International Comparison Approach (Paris, OECD, 1970).

OECD: Educational Policies for the 1970s (Paris, OECD, 1971).

V. Onushkin: The Role of Universities in Post-Experience Higher Education (Paris, IIEP, 1974).

H.S. Parnes: Forecasting Educational Needs for Economic and Social Development (Paris, OECD, 1962).

J. Poorter: "Vraag en aanbod van artsen in het jaar 2000", in Medisch Contact, Vol. 32, pp. 269-273.

H. Riese: Die Entwicklung des Bedarfs an Hochschulabsolventen in der Bundesrepublik Deutschland (Wiesbaden, Steiner, 1967).

T. Schaefer and J. Wahse: Die Bestimmung des Kaderbedarfs nach Fachrichtungen und Qualifikationsstufen mit Hilfe eines Regressionsmodells (1977).

V. Stoikov: "Recurrent education: some neglected economic issues", in International Labour Review, Vol. 108, Nos. 2-3, pp. 187-209.

T. Thorstad: Manual for Education Projections (Paris, UNESCO, forthcoming).

M. Trow: "Problems in the transition from élite to mass higher education", in Policies for Higher Education (Paris, OECD, 1974; OECD General Report).

UNESCO: Statistical Yearbook 1965 (Paris, UNESCO, 1965).

UNESCO: Statistical Yearbook 1975 (Paris, UNESCO 1976).

UNESCO: Education Statistics - Latest Year Available (Paris, UNESCO, 1977).

G.L. Williams: Towards a Lifelong Education: A New Role for Higher Education Institutions (Paris, UNESCO, 1977).

P. de Wolff: "Employment forecasting techniques in the Netherlands", in Employment Forecasting (Paris, OECD, 1963).

Worsa: Wetenschappelijk onderwijs raming studentenaantallen 1975-90 (Amsterdam, Ministry of Education and Science, 1975).